THERE'S SOMETHING ABOUT MARY

The Rollercoaster Tale of a Sixties Hippy Chick

MARY MURDOCH

Ghost Writer and Editor: Sherron Mayes, The Editing Den

For Dave

ACKNOWLEDGMENTS

This book would not be here without the encouragement from my dear friend, Rosheen Finnigan, and the patience of my ghost writer and editor, Sherron Mayes, who deciphered my scribblings and spent many hours interviewing me to capture the full story of my life.

CONTENTS

FORWARD

Dear Reader,

First, I want to thank you for picking up my book. I'm not a celebrity, although some might say, I was a local superstar back in the seventies! But more of that later. In the meantime, I bet you're wondering who I am. So, let me introduce myself.

I'm Mary Murdoch and I've been married twice, so formerly known as Mary Browning, and christened Mary Doody. And I guess, I'm just an ordinary seventy-one-year-old woman, although still as sharp as a tack, and may I say, still in good shape 😊

Some folks from my past might describe me as an adrenaline junkie and add that I'm far too generous and caring, sacrificing my life needlessly. Others might say, I was selfish and impulsive at times, seeing life through rose-tinted specs. The truth is, I'm just a former hippy chick who grabbed the sixties by the throat and lived a rollercoaster life packed full of drama, fun, grief, and sadness – but most of all LOVE.

So, dear Reader, I know we're strangers right now. But I hope by the end of this book, after experiencing all my ups and downs, you'll consider me a friend.

PART 1

DAD

I know that I'm a prisoner
To all my father held so dear
I know that I'm a hostage
To all his hopes and fears
I just wish I could have told him in the living years

CHAPTER ONE

My Not So Grand Entrance

I was born in Windrush Camp, Gloucestershire on the 7th March, 1951. To be frank, it was a right dump – an abandoned airfield owned by the RAF once used during the war as a relief landing ground. My parents worked for the Air Ministry, and somehow, they ended up being the chief cooks and bottle washers for displaced people after the second world war. And along with everyone else, we lived in hideous one-bed prefabs which looked like mini-bungalows with tin and asbestos roofs. My parents, along with me and my brother, Pat, who was three years my senior, all slept in one room, which was so damp that water dripped down the walls. It was like being incarcerated in a cell with no release date.

Four years later, good fortune finally smiled on us – our damp, mouldy dwelling was so unhabitual that it was due for demolition. Hooray! We were given priority housing, along with all the families from the camp. Standing with our luggage in long queues, we were bussed out to Melville council estate just on the edge of Bourton-on-the Water, a village in the rural Cotswolds.

On arrival, we all clambered off the bus and walked up to the entrance of our new three-bed house with my dad jangling the front door keys and my brother and I jumping up and down with excitement at finally having a proper home like normal people.

The buff-coloured building needed a thorough clean inside but Mum said that was easily remedied – and we didn't mind, we had the perfect play area – a sixty-foot-long back garden. It was overgrown with weeds and nettles but paradise to us kids as Pat and I raced outside to explore this new green space.

Within a few months, Mum had the house sorted, and Father had tamed the garden and started a vegetable patch growing beans, cabbages, potatoes, and carrots.

Life seemed to be heading in a positive direction. Or so we thought…

CHAPTER TWO

Booze-Fuelled Rages

Before I continue, let me tell you about my parents – Audrey and James.

Mum was one of four girls from a well-heeled family in Buckinghamshire, and looking at old photos, she was a bit of a head turner being five foot six and slim with curly dark hair. She met my father when they both worked in a Lancashire hotel – Mum as a chambermaid and Dad as a cook. And they got closer after going for drinks after work. It wasn't long after that she was preggers with my older brother, Pat.

My mother was a wonderful woman and twenty years younger than my father. You might say they were the total opposites like muck and brass, black and white, yin and yang etc, so, in all honesty, I don't think they were ever a love match. The facts were, Mum was a much younger girl who got pregnant, and in that era, Dad would have felt obliged to marry her. And like many couples back then, they muddled on to keep the family together unlike today's quickie divorces.

Anyway, back to Mum. I'll always remember her with a wraparound apron over her clothes where she was either cleaning or cooking unless she was in her Sunday best for church. And she was the loveliest person, always there with a smile, teaching Pat and me to read and write before we went to school. Money was tight, but she'd take us out for walks, pointing out flowers and trees, and then we'd go foraging for raspberries and blackberries and she'd make crumbles, cakes, and trifles with the fruit. So, there was always the aroma of something delicious when we came home from school. She even made her own elderberry wine.

Dad was Irish, the eldest of ten, and a strict Catholic, so I was baptised quickly after my birth. He believed that an unbaptised child was sent to purgatory after death, so you can imagine the religious indoctrination we kids were subject to.

He was fifty-three when I was born, so I always knew him as having grey hair and seeming much older than other kids' fathers. "Is that your grandad?" other children would shout if they saw me and Pat with him. But despite his age, he was still a handsome man, a six-footer who cut a bit of an eccentric figure, walking around proudly in a second-hand suit with a trilby hat perched on his head at a jaunty angle. He'd hold a shillelagh (a wooden walking stick) in his right hand which he didn't need, but I think it gave him a sense of prestige.

After our move, Dad headed straight to his new job as a clerk at the RAF station in Little Rissington, just up the road. Mum was pleased to bits that he'd be earning more money, but unfortunately, every Friday when he got paid, he'd spend most of his wages on beer and whiskey, and his booze-fuelled rants began to terrify the living daylights out of us.

We'd all sit around the kitchen table waiting for him to arrive home from work so we could start eating dinner. Eventually, when it was obvious, he wasn't coming back anytime soon, Mum told us to tuck in while she'd go without, not wanting to cause a row. We soon realised, it was when the pubs closed at ten, that he'd stumble through the door shouting and balling at my mother, waking me and my brother up. At the age of five, I still shared a room with Pat, so I'd nervously climb out of my bed and into his, and we'd cling to each other, shit scared, and trembling under the covers.

One Saturday night, we heard Dad barge his way into the house, hollering at the top of his voice, threatening this and that. "You're a whore," he shouted at our mother, "If it wasn't for me, you'd still be in the gutter."

I remember crying as I ran to the top of the stairs, my heart pounding with fear of what might happen next. My mother would react as if she was on red alert and usher me and my brother into the bedroom wardrobe where we hid amongst all the clothes, mothballs hitting us in the face. Sometimes we'd be in there for an hour, waiting with bated breath until things calmed down until finally, Mum came and got us saying that Father had passed out on the sofa.

The following morning, he'd be very remorseful. "I don't know what came over me," he'd mutter over breakfast. "It won't happen again." And then as a religious zealot, he'd take us to church on a Sunday, go to confession and offload his guilt. Even at that age, I found it hypocritical that Dad could torment us all with his outbursts and still be instantly cleansed of all his sins.

Father's abusive screaming continued every weekend, telling us all we weren't good enough or accusing us of something or other. As a consequence, those emotional wounds were carved deep, and I grew up desperate to escape.

Mother never discussed his drunken behaviour with us, so I don't know if he physically struck her as she was always covered up with long sleeves or skirts. I always worried about how he behaved with her when they were alone, but in those days, it would be undignified for a woman to reveal too much about her marriage, especially to her children.

The morning after one of Dad's volatile outbursts, I'd always go to my parents individually, throwing my arms around my mum and asking if she was okay. And then I'd do the same with Dad, treading on eggshells, to see if he needed anything. I just wanted them to be happy, so that life could get back to normal. I guess I was scared that otherwise, things would escalate and something terrible would happen.

I now realise that this was when my role as healer, counsellor, and peacemaker began – a role I've played my entire life, putting others first, and sacrificing my own needs.

CHAPTER THREE

Unbreak My Heart

Six months after we moved in, Dad brought a dog into the house. I watched it excitedly as it wandered around, nosing into every corner of the kitchen. Who knows where he got it from, maybe it was a stray, but I was delighted, and we named him Bunny. And that gorgeous creature – a cross between a sheep dog and a collie – proved to be my salvation.

Having a pet is so healing, so whilst snuggling up with him on my bed, I shared all my heartache about my father's volatile outbursts. The poor thing had also witnessed my father's verbal abuse and even got the odd kick from him when Dad was in full swing with his endless accusations. Bunny would gaze at me with his chocolate button eyes, and somehow, I felt he understood. There was this incredible bond between us, and I can honestly say, hand on heart, that it was the first time in my life, that I'd felt unconditional love. Over the next six years, he became my antidote against all the relentless arguing.

Then something happened to rip apart my warm, fuzzy bubble.

One Sunday morning, I was due to go to church, but Bunny was nowhere to be seen. Apparently, Dad had let him out the back door the previous day and he was left roaming around the streets. "I'm not going anywhere," I said sadly, "until we find Bunny."

Not long after, there was a knock at the door. Dad opened it, and as I stood behind him anxiously, I heard a man say, "Your dog has been run over. He's on the side of the main road."

At this point, I didn't know whether Bunny was dead or alive, but I started sobbing as Father dashed out to bring him home. I was trembling like a leaf as I stood outside the front door, praying that Bunny was okay. But as my stomach churned, I feared the worst.

Dad returned twenty minutes later with Bunny lying in his arms. My dear, trusted friend, the keeper of all my secrets, was dead. Wrapping him in a blanket, he set him down on the lawn at the bottom of the garden as I watched with tears rolling down my cheeks. Still staring at Bunny with wet eyes, I lay beside him cuddling his limp body. Soon after, Dad buried him in a private space in the garden where he was surrounded by gooseberry and blackcurrant bushes.

I was distraught. What would I do now? How would I survive? He was my only confidant. I had no stability in our family life, always looking over my shoulder on tenterhooks because of Dad's reign of terror. And I couldn't confide in my mum having seen her cry too many times to mention. I was close to my brother, Pat, but he was often out somewhere, wandering around the fields, bird watching or collecting dead mice or insects. When we were together, we often communicated with a look of silent dread, too scared to speak in case we said the wrong thing.

I was wandering up and down our road crying when Stephen came along on a push-along scooter. He stopped, stared at me, and mumbled. I looked up and there was this silent connection between us as if he understood exactly how I was feeling. I soon discovered he was sixteen, so six years older than me, which would have been frowned on for a ten-year-old girl, but he had Downs Syndrome, and because of his learning disabilities he had the mental age of a five-year-old.

Together, we sat on a little wall outside my house, and my grief over losing my darling doggie tumbled out. And even though Steven couldn't speak properly, he held my hand and gazed into my eyes so lovingly, it felt much more powerful than words.

For many months, we were inseparable. As he scooted around the estate, I'd run alongside him as the other kids pointed and yelled out 'spastic' or 'mongol,' but I ignored them. I didn't care that he was disabled. What I loved was that he was uncomplicated and only focused on the moment we were in. And that was a welcome distraction from my grief.

Then suddenly he disappeared too.

I felt confused, searching for him around the area, wondering what had happened to him. "It's strange that he's not around," I said to my mum.

Then she told me what she'd heard. "Steven's dead, darling," she answered as she touched my hair.

The blood drained from my face. I was devastated and ran upstairs to my room and lay in bed sobbing under the bedclothes. Why had he died? He was so young. I knew he had Down's syndrome and there were other complications, but it felt so unfair.

Then, thankfully, another new pal appeared, albeit much older. Miss Francis, a spinster in her eighties, lived a few doors down from us. My mum started doing some cleaning for her, and I'd tag along. She was very wrinkled, her hands contorted with arthritis, but despite being almost blind, she created some beautiful, crocheted work, such as cardigans, hats, and scarves.

You might think it strange that as a young girl, I saw a grandmotherly figure as a friend, but I didn't define friendship by age. I was always drawn to someone's spirit rather than their appearance.

It became a routine that on the way home from school, I'd call in to make her a cuppa, and after, I'd sit beside her on the settee as she taught me to crochet. But somehow, she sensed that something wasn't right. Perhaps Mum confided in her, but several times she asked me, "Is everything all right at home?"

I smiled and said, "Yeah, fine, thanks." Of course, that was a lie. But I felt it was disloyal to tell our family secrets. And she didn't question me further.

Then one day, months later, I knocked, and she didn't answer, despite me calling out her name. I kept banging on the door and then bent down to peer through the letter box but couldn't see anything. Worried sick, I ran home and told my mum that Miss Francis wasn't answering. Mum looked at me sadly and then grabbed my hands, "Sorry, darling," she said softly, "but Miss Francis has died."

Once more my eyes welled with tears. "Another person dead. But why," I gasped. "Why do I keep losing people that I've grown to care for?"

"Life is like that Mary," Mum replied. "We're here one minute and gone the next."

Both my mother's parents, her uncle and her sister all died from T.B. when she was eleven, so I guess she'd somehow adjusted to loss and grief. But I was too young to adjust to it. And I was frightened of losing anyone else.

My way of dealing with things was to paint on a smile until the sadness overwhelmed me and I couldn't fight the turmoil any longer. Then I started having fainting fits. I knew deep down it was my body's reaction to all this trauma. I remember standing in church singing a hymn feeling woozy and then I passed out, only to come round to a crowd of people staring down at me.

Another time, I was in school assembly when I slumped onto the floor and lost consciousness. Eventually, the seizures got so bad, occurring two to three times a week, that I was taken to a specialist hospital in Oxford by ambulance. Whilst there, I had electrodes attached to my head to measure my brain activity and then given medication, and thankfully, the seizures stopped. But the grief in my heart never left me.

CHAPTER FOUR

Mr Tombs

Around this time, we became acquainted with Mr and Mrs Tombs, our next-door neighbours. They had three teenage daughters who would regularly walk me to school. Mr Tombs was stocky, tall, grey-haired and had Parkinson's disease, so his hands would constantly tremble. However, his wife, Mrs Tombs, was quite the opposite – a formidable figure, short and skinny with a pinched face. She was always telling us off for something, especially for throwing tennis balls around the garden, so I only went over there when she was working.

As you can imagine, Pat and I preferred Mr Tombs by far. He was a kind, happy man who always hugged me when we left the house just as he did with his daughters. He also kept chickens in their back garden. One day he killed one of them for Sunday lunch while Pat was watching over the fence. To my brother's delight, Mr Tombs handed him the chicken feet, explaining how Pat could make them move by pulling on the tendon. That was a big mistake – Pat chased me around the garden with the disgusting feet in his hands as I screamed, "Get away from me."

That was typical of my brother and grisly antics. His bedroom was like a science lab where he kept loads of dead birds, mice, butterflies, and moths in his chest of drawers, so he could dissect them with a pocketknife. He also kept the skulls of foxes, badgers, and rats. Later on in life, he became an environmentalist, so that explains a lot.

Anyway, back to Mr Tombs. One weekend, after arriving home from playing in the woods with my brother and his friends our mum ran out of the house and bundled the two of us upstairs, pushing us into the 'safety' wardrobe in my bedroom. We didn't need to ask why. Dad was back from the pub, stomping around the house like a bull on steroids, shouting, "HOW'S YOUR FANCY MAN, MR TOMBS? I KNOW WHAT'S GOING ON, YOU HUSSY, YOU WHORE."

Mum, her eyes wide with panic and breathing heavily pushed a chest of drawers against the bedroom door as we all trembled with fear. Time ticked by as we all stood there in the darkness hearing Dad still banging about, screaming about Mr Tombs. "COME HERE YOU SLUT."

I remember putting my hand over my mouth in shock. Surely this couldn't be true – were Mr Tombs and Mum having an affair? Or was this Dad's paranoia? I still have no idea to this day what happened. I only know that we weren't allowed to speak to any of the family again.

The Tombs must have heard the drama through the walls as they quickly erected a fence between our gardens to ensure we couldn't enter. It was sad. We missed having them in our lives.

CHAPTER FIVE

Escape to the Farm

Pat left home at eighteen after attaining a place at Sussex University and there was suddenly an even bigger gap in my life. On the plus side, I was now able to move into his larger bedroom where I could feel close to him somehow. He was always my ally against Dad and my protector. When boys picked on me, he'd always stand up for me, shouting, "Leave my sister alone?" I didn't even mind seeing all the dead creatures he left behind, because he'd also left me his record player, transistor radio and a Cilla Black record, 'Anyone who had a Heart.' I played that song over and over.

After a few weeks, I wrote to him, but he'd didn't reply. I assumed he was busy studying, making new friends and working in a bar in the evenings. But it still hurt. And now, I was left alone to deal with our volatile father.

Dad had retired and was drinking much more heavily than before which made him even more verbally abusive. He'd get up around lunchtime and head straight to the local pub and then return home to scream at us all. But Dad was as equally obsessed with the church as he was alcohol, reciting biblical phrases to us at every mealtime when he could command my attention.

Because of his strict religious beliefs, I'd already had my first Communion at the age of ten where you commit yourself to God. And at the age of fourteen, I had my Confirmation to complete my initiation into the church and deepen my personal relationship with God.

Initially, I was excited, especially when I was given a new white dress and veil for these very special occasions as well as a bible written in Latin and a St. Christopher medal to keep me safe from harm. But I also had to confess my sins regularly; something I came to detest. It's as if you're being programmed to believe that we're all riddled with a darkness that only a priest can eliminate. *Bless me Father for I have sinned since my last confession. Blah! Blah!* What sins did I need to confess as a young girl?

1. Answering my parent's back.
2. Not coming in when called for dinner.
3. Using God's name in vain and on and on.

But apparently, I needed a punishment, so I'd have to say ten Hail Marys and ten Our Fathers and then spend a week going straight to bed after our evening meal.

But then Father started taking things one step further.

"When you become a nun, you'll be happier and closer to God," he'd say over the dinner table as he was slicing through a piece of steak and kidney pie. "You'll be with other young girls knowing that you'll all be destined for heaven."

He started slipping comments like this into the conversation all the time and I soon realised what he was really grooming me for – and it wasn't about being close to God. He wanted me locked away so no man could defile his precious daughter. And as a young girl, dreaming of finding a soul mate, I wasn't remotely interested. It may be the path to salvation for some, but to me, it meant no chance of marriage or even friendships. I'd just be stuck in a building with a load of other lonely women. The threat was terrifying like a guillotine hanging over me. I had visions of him bundling me onto a bus in the middle of the night and dumping me outside a convent.

"No way am I going to end up a nun," I said to my mum one morning before Dad woke up.

"You know what your dad's like. He's all talk, so don't worry about it," she'd say.

Either way, Mum decided with my brother gone, that it was best if I wasn't left alone with Dad. So, during the six-week summer break, she asked my friend, Tessa's parents, if I could spend the holidays on their huge dairy farm just up the road. I'd known Tessa since primary school; she was one of my besties since the age of five. I can still remember her all these years later as if it was yesterday – slim with olive skin and elfin dark hair.

I was overjoyed when her parents said yes, thrilled to be out of the family home. And wow, did I make some amazing memories, herding the cows for milking, mucking out the cow sheds, haymaking, and driving the tractor. We even went to agricultural sales with Tessa's dad.

Some evenings they had crayfish parties that the entire family and neighbouring farmers attended. The men would put the nets out in the river, and then collect the little rock lobsters in a bucket. They'd stoke up a bonfire and boil a pot of water which was suspended over the flames that the crayfish would be thrown into. Everyone would bring something such as salad, homemade bread, and fruitcake along with beer for the grownups and homemade lemonade for us kids. After we'd eaten, we'd play games and sing our hearts out. It was real family fun. A sharp contrast to life back home.

PART 2

BILL

And they called it puppy love
Just because we're seventeen
Tell them all, please tell them it isn't fair
To take away my only dream

CHAPTER SIX

Tech College and a Handsome Boy

At the age of seventeen, I started tech college, along with my friend Christine to learn the genius art of secretarial work. And this time, we pledged to be more responsible.

Two years earlier, Christine and I had gone to evening classes to learn to type. Her parents owned Pulhams Coaches – a bus and coach hire company – so while they were still out working, after school, we'd raid the larder, nibbling on fig rolls and rich tea biscuits. And then with great excitement, we'd open their drink cabinet in the living room, and neck back glasses of Cinzano and lemonade.

Afterwards, we staggered in late to our typing class, tipsy and reeking of booze as the teacher stared at us disapprovingly. Then she gave us a big sniff, inhaling our alcoholic aroma, and threatened to send a letter of complaint to our parents.

Red-faced, we apologised profusely. We didn't want to get into trouble, but like most rebellious teens, we didn't want to stop our antics either. So, we made sure that we brushed our teeth and sprayed on some of Christine's mother's perfume after any more Cinzano binges.

But back to Tech College. By a stroke of luck, Christine and I ended up in the same class. Our first lesson was on Pitman's shorthand, which could have been Egyptian hieroglyphics as far as we were concerned. It was quite the challenge for both of us as we could never get our heads around all the coded squiggles. Thankfully, another student, called Carolyn Sweet sat behind us with her friend Margaret Daft. After studying shorthand for six months at school, she helped us out until we caught up.

The four of us struck up a great friendship until my eyes fell on the most gorgeous guy I'd ever seen. His name was Bill, a striking six-footer with thick, black hair and a heartbreaking smile. I soon discovered he was two years older than me at nineteen and studying to become an airline pilot.

It seemed like fate when we kept bumping into one another in the corridors, and whenever I saw him, I blushed profusely. I was so shy around him that I was truly gobsmacked when he finally asked me out.

Standing with my girlfriends in the gardens of the college, he asked if he could have a word. In breathless excitement, I stuttered out a yes. But afterwards, I wondered if he was just having a joke at my expense. I'd always been the ugly duckling at junior school and called specky four eyes and spotty. Now, I had the attention of the best-looking bloke in college, and once I got chatting with him, I realised he was also sophisticated, well-mannered and kind.

On our first date, he took me to see a Disney film at the cinema. Buying us both popcorn and a Fanta orange, he sat beside me with his arm around my shoulders. I was so nervous, I barely watched the movie, but when it finished, he leaned over and kissed me. I couldn't believe it. My very first smooch from a boy. I was walking on air.

A week later, his parents invited me over for dinner and I was awestruck. They had a fancy four-bed detached property, and I was shocked when I walked inside. It was like a showhouse. They were super-posh, so I wanted to make a good impression, washing up afterwards in a very organised manner – glasses first, cutlery, then crockery – hoping his parents thought I was good wife material. I certainly wanted to give that impression.

A few months after going there for dinner every week, I was invited to stay overnight. Naturally, Bill and I weren't allowed to sleep together in his parent's house, so I shared a room with his younger sister, who was around my age, where there were two single beds.

Bill shared a room with his young brother, but on that first sleepover, I was desperate to snuggle up to my lovely boyfriend. So, when everyone had gone to bed, I'd check his sister was asleep, and then sneak along the corridor to his room, going past their Collie dog, Tansy, sleeping in the hallway, praying she wouldn't bark. Thankfully, Tansy sat there quietly, giving me the all-clear to steal in beside Bill so we could kiss and cuddle for a bit. God knows whether his ten-year-old brother was awake or not as we were oblivious to anything but each other. If he was awake, he never told on us.

After everything that had happened, I was thrilled that a new life beckoned with a loving boyfriend and his close family. I'd never met my grandparents, but his grandma lived with them too. I'd take her in a piece of fruit cake to her bedsitting room where she often ate alone if she was tired. It was wonderful to sit and chat with her about the war and her childhood and she often told me that I was really good for Bill.

CHAPTER SEVEN

The Proposal

After six months of dating, Bill asked me to marry him in a nearby park. We sat on a bench by a big oak tree, and he did the old-fashioned thing and got down on one knee. Then he slipped a diamond ring onto my finger. It was stunning with five stones inset into eighteen-carat gold. I was over the moon. He'd spent one hundred pounds on it; a lot of money in those days. But most importantly, it meant he was committed to our relationship.

Those were the heady days of young love filled with walks from my house to the Slaughters – a pretty Cotswold village with babbling brooks where we'd go for picnics with his dog, Tansy. We often sat in one of the fields where cows were grazing nearby and tucked into a picnic basket full of food that his mum prepared – a mixture of egg and cress, cheese and cucumber sandwiches, homemade scones, crisps, and lemonade.

One night after our end-of-term college dance, we lay on damp grass in the grounds, the glorious blue sky above permitting us to smooch and canoodle. But we didn't make love, intending to save ourselves for marriage.

But before we walked down the aisle, we needed to save up. Bill had taken a live-in summer job with wayward youngsters in care whilst he waited to go to flying school. And I'd just got a job as a secretary in a solicitor's office. Life couldn't get any better. Bill had already taught me to drive in his grey van and I was amazed when I passed my test the first time. I'd borrow his vehicle during the week to go to work and then visit him at the weekends, staying in a spare bed in the 'wayward girls' dormitory. However, there was a formidable matron there, so as much as I wanted to sneak in with him as I'd done at his family home, I didn't dare. We were, after all, meant to set an example to the youngsters.

After a year of dating, Bill and I were officially engaged, and his parents insisted on meeting with my mother and father at our family home, probably to check out my background, and whether or not, I really was daughter-in-law material.

Needless to say, I was worried sick. Bill's parent's house was glossy middle-class perfection, whereas ours was a dirty tip, despite my mum being a cleaner. By the time she got home, she was too tired to dust and hoover anymore.

What would his Mum and Dad think of our cheap lino in the hallway, threadbare carpets and an old red sofa stuffed with horsehair that was spilling out? To top it all, there was a constant aroma of booze and snuff, courtesy of my father, which still, after all these decades later, makes my stomach churn if I smell it. And I prayed hard that Dad wouldn't sit opposite them with tobacco cascading down his nose.

I wasn't so concerned about what Bill thought. He'd been to my house many times, but he seemed so infatuated with me, that he never appeared to notice the state of the place or at least, he never said anything. But I knew his posh parents would take everything in.

"Mum," I said, the day before they were due, "we can't let them see it like this. We've got to do a hardcore clean."

She agreed but the place was in such a state, we just focused on the hallway and the living room. Although, I didn't know what to do if they used our yucky toilet.

It was a Saturday, and they were due at 4 pm. Mum barely had any decent clothes, but she managed to find a nice summer dress in her wardrobe, and dad put on his smart church clothes.

When Bill's parents finally arrived, I was nervous as hell. Bill's dad, an ex-RAF squadron leader, was suited and booted, his hair gelled back. His mother was in an expensive dress and bolero jacket, her short hair styled at the hairdressers and carrying a green hat that matched her handbag and shoes.

My mum was nervous too, meeting my fiancé's parents for the first time, knowing that my dad was still hoping I'd become a nun. He'd already got into a rage about me being engaged, stating I was too young. But Mum told him straight. "Come on, James, she's a woman now and can do as she pleases."

When Bill's parents entered the living room, I was on tenterhooks waiting for a reaction, and sure enough, his mother gave his father a look as if to say, what have we walked into? But they were too polite to comment.

Mum had gone all out and baked a fruit cake and there was a teapot on the table with cheap unmatched cups. We didn't have much. Previously, Dad had sold our dinner service for beer money, and we never had enough cash to replace anything.

After introductions, Bill and I went for a walk, as our parents wanted to talk privately. We got back half an hour later, and I heard from Mum later that compromises were made – my father, Mr Religious with a capital R, insisted that despite not getting married in a church, any future children of ours had to be brought up as Catholics. We appeared to have no say in this. Did we care? Not a lot. We were in love, and we knew we'd eventually do things our own way.

But things changed after that. I clearly wasn't quite the well-brought-up young lady Bill's mum and dad first thought as they were a little more distant when I went over there. But I didn't give two hoots. Bill was heading off to flying school down in Southampton to secure our future. I was engaged to this gorgeous Adonis and had a good job. Life was getting better and better.

Up the Junction

Before he went off to flying school, Bill drove us to Brighton for my brother Pat's twenty-first birthday bash. Pat was now a handsome six-footer, having turned into a cool hippy with long hair. It was a wild party with the entire three-story Georgian house full of students from Sussex University playing music and having fun. Bill and I danced and kissed surrounded by crowds of people.

The following day, we explored Brighton and walked around all the market stalls in the lanes. And that night, we made love for the first time on the famous shingle beach. Yes, I know what you're thinking – I mentioned earlier that we'd wait for marriage to do the deed, but we were crazy about each other. And in our defence, we'd drunk a fair bit of beer, and were madly in love.

Afterwards, we walked back to my brother's place grinning from ear to ear, feeling a fuzzy new-found bond, that we'd sealed the deal.

On arrival, the house was still packed with students sprawled everywhere, and music was blasting out, but my brother had offered us his bed, and later that night, we made love again – so, I'd officially lost my cherry good and proper.

Back home, a few weeks later, whilst still learning about my junior secretarial job, my monthly period didn't arrive. I was stressed out, to say the least. Desperate to get away from the controlling clutches of my father, there was no way that I wanted the responsibility of a child.

Naturally, I confided in Bill. Sick with worry, he told his parents and apparently, they went berserk and shouted at him – "She'll have to have an abortion, otherwise, you'll ruin your career before it's even got started, not accounting for how this will destroy Mary's job prospects."

I cried when he told me how they'd reacted, but I agreed it was for the best. Abortion wasn't legal then, but Bill's mother was a retired nurse, so she handed him some pills to give me. Keeping it a secret from my parents, I swallowed them back with a large gin, and throughout the night I had severe cramping pains, vomiting continually. When I bled, to my relief, it was all over.

But the slippery slope had begun.

Bill went off to the flying school in Southampton and I missed him like mad. He'd come home once or twice a month but after the pregnancy, I was never invited back to his family home. Bill became more distant too, popping over to meet me from work, but then saying he had to dash off. I guess I knew deep down that we were finished, but at that point, I was still very much in love with him and didn't want to face the truth.

CHAPTER EIGHT

She's Leaving Home

I hated living at home with my father as he continued to shove his religious views down my throat, along with criticising everything I did. He demanded that I give him three-quarters of my wage, which I knew would only be spent on booze, and I couldn't go out in the evening without him making a scene if I wasn't back by a ten o'clock curfew.

Naturally, like most teens, I wanted to rebel and make the best of myself. So, I grew my chestnut hair long and showcased my hourglass figure in Mary Quant black and white dresses. The sight of me glammed up certainly got Father's hackles up which caused more screaming rows. But then it seriously kicked off when I got home in the early hours, trying to sneak in through the front door. Dad was waiting up and instantly went bonkers, his face beetroot red, his fists clenched, "WHERE HAVE YOU BEEN, YOU WHORE. YOU'RE A SLUT JUST LIKE YOUR MOTHER! GET OUT OF MY HOUSE NOW AND DON'T DARKEN MY DOORSTEP AGAIN."

Mum quickly appeared from upstairs, her face as white as a sheet. "Best go up to your bedroom, love, and I'll sort this out."

But I'd had enough of the abuse, and finally dared to stand up to him. "Don't worry, Dad, I'm going. I'll leave tomorrow."

Standing there in his dressing gown looking dishevelled, Dad glared at me and then snapped, "Fine, but I want you out of here first thing."

After a sleepless night worrying about where I was going to live, the next morning I packed a suitcase, hugged Mum goodbye and jumped on a bus, as usual, to head to work. Despite the uncertainty of my future, I was relieved to be out of that toxic environment. But beggars can't be choosers, so I was more than happy to sofa surf or sleep on a friend's floor if I had to. But whose door could I knock on? Then I thought of Eddie, an old friend from college. He was a ten-minute walk from the solicitor's office, so when I clocked off, I headed over there with all my belongings.

I'd visited him many times before, and once he heard what had happened, he let me stay for a few nights until his girlfriend appeared. She was an attractive Eastern European with blonde curly hair and bright blue eyes. And she clearly had a jealous streak.

"What are you doing here?" she asked, her eyes narrowed.

"I'm just staying for a few days," I replied with a smile.

Fortunately, I'd been scouring the local newspaper for rentals and found a ground-floor bedsit in a Victorian terrace for five shillings a week. It was, shall we say, cosy. There was a bedroom/kitchenette with two single beds and a bay window that looked out onto the road. On the landing, I shared a bathroom with a couple upstairs who had a kid. Two lads lived in the basement.

After I unpacked, I wrote to Bill to explain that I'd moved into my own place, hoping it would make him want to spend more time with me. A few weeks after, he turned up unexpectedly on a Saturday morning. Feeling elated at seeing him on my doorstep, I invited him in hoping everything would get back on track between us.

"Fancy a cuppa?" I said with a smile.

"No thanks, I'm not staying," he answered as he fiddled nervously with the sleeve of his shirt.

My stomach lurched. I couldn't bear to hear what was coming.

He looked at me earnestly. "I'm sorry, Mary, but I've met someone else."

I discovered it was a girl he met back in tech college where we'd both got together. And I knew exactly who she was — tall and elegant, she was stunningly beautiful like a model in a magazine, and she talked just like Joanna Lumley with a cut glass accent.

I didn't cry or plead with him. I guess I wasn't surprised that he didn't want me. I wasn't in the same league as her. But after he left, I sobbed my heart out which I continued to do every night for the next week. Now and then, I'd gaze sadly at the engagement ring on my finger, a symbol of the future we might have had. I couldn't bear to get rid of it, finally taking it off and keeping it in a jewellery box with all my brooches and earrings. After all, he was my first real love, the man I lost my virginity to, so it felt like a bereavement.

I told Mum, and as usual, she visited, bringing over some groceries so I wouldn't starve. But with no phones, and feeling lonely and sorry for myself, I wrote to my brother about my breakup. It had been a few months since I'd seen him at his birthday party when Bill and I had made love and thrown a grenade onto the fire. And bless Pat's heart, he drove up the following weekend in a mini-van with a friend.

When he knocked on the door, I was overjoyed to see him, which put my heartbreak out of my mind for a while. We hugged, and he said, "It's all right kiddo, your big brother's here."

After eating toast for dinner to save money, we went out for drinks in the local pub. His advice was always practical: "That's life kiddo, suck it up and move on." If only it was that simple. The next morning, they left after a cuppa and another slice of toast and I felt a little less alone in the world, but I was desperately worried about money. I was proud of myself for finding my own accommodation, but I earned just over six shillings a week and after paying five shillings rent, I wasn't left with much.

Then Eddie told me his girlfriend needed somewhere to live. She asked if she could move in, and despite her being uppity when I first met her, I said yes, immediately, grateful that we could share, so I'd have some leftover cash for groceries.

But that didn't last long. A fortnight later, I came home after work to find that she'd disappeared leaving all her stuff. After a week went by, there was still no sign of her. These days, I would have reported it to the police if a young girl had disappeared leaving all their things behind, but back then, it was the 'Turn on, Tune in, Drop out' philosophy of the sixties and people were often fly-by-nights.

I told Eddie that she'd disappeared, and he was as puzzled as me as to where she'd gone, but he knew I had to find another roommate, so he came by and picked up her stuff to clear the decks. Meanwhile, I was living on jam sandwiches.

CHAPTER NINE

The Attack

A month later, with no roomie, I discovered the challenges of being a girl on her own. It was still August summertime, so as usual, I walked to my bedsit after work around five. I was only a few minutes away from home when I turned into an alleyway and heard footsteps behind me.

"Hello, pretty girl. Fancy a fuck?" said a gravelly voice.

I turned my head and saw a man with ginger hair coming towards me. He must have been mid-twenties and at least six feet tall. My heart was in my throat as I yelled, "GO AWAY! LEAVE ME ALONE!"

I broke into a run, but he caught up with me, grabbing me around the neck and shoulders. Fortunately, a few years back, I'd learnt judo at a youth club, and I reacted instinctively from all my training, bending forwards, taking his weight on my back, and then throwing him over. He hit the ground with a thud. And as he lay there, groaning in pain, I finished him off with a kick to his nuts and quickly turned and sprinted towards my front door.

Grabbing the keys from my handbag, I fumbled with the lock as my hands were shaking so much. Once inside, I closed the curtains and slumped on my bed, my heart still racing. I was worried that he'd followed me, and I felt so isolated and alone. I had no telephone to call the police and no Bill to talk to, and I felt too ashamed to say anything to my new neighbours considering I'd only moved in a few weeks earlier.

Over the next few days, I was too scared to leave the house for work in case that psycho was lying in wait. I just lay on my bed, sobbing with Radio Luxembourg blasting out music for company. I got no sleep at all, my thoughts whirling around chaotically as I kept getting up to check that the door and windows were locked.

When I finally opened the curtains after three days, my attacker walked past my window waving at me with a creepy grin. I was terrified. My worst fears had come true. This weirdo knew where I lived! Worse still, for the rest of that week, he stalked me daily, walking past several times a day with that same horrible smile.

Would he find a way to break in, try and rape and murder me?

What should I do? Move back home to my first hell?

While I was still in my room having barely eaten, a knock at my door startled me.

"Hello, are you there? I'm Ruth from upstairs," a woman yelled.

I got up anxiously and answered, looking dishevelled and drained from lack of sleep and worry.

"Hi," she said with a look of concern. "I haven't seen you around much. Are you OK?" She had a mumsy vibe and was holding the hand of her daughter, a little blonde girl around five.

Initially, I put on a brave face. "Yes," I replied, "I'm fine, thank you."

But somehow, she knew I was lying. Looking at me sympathetically, she asked, "Can I come in?"

I nodded, and with her and her daughter following behind, something inside me cracked open, and I slumped down on my bed and started crying uncontrollably.

"Oh, love, tell me what happened?" Ruth said as she sat on the mattress beside me and rubbed my shoulder.

When I finally calmed down, I told her about the attack, and in response, she looked at me with concern. "Mary, this man is dangerous. You must go to the police."

I needed some wise guidance and after a little persuasion, I dared to venture back outside as she and her daughter accompanied me to the local police station.

I was with the cops for a good hour, giving a full account of what happened whilst Ruth waited outside. As I was under eighteen, the police still considered me a minor, so they took me back to my parents in Bourton-on-the-water despite me pleading that I was fine. I was dreading that Dad might insist I stay until I was legally an adult which was in another six months' time. I couldn't bear the thought. But thankfully, I needn't have worried. Dad didn't want me there, so with his signed consent, the police took me back to my studio in Cheltenham.

After taking five days off, I finally went back to work and was promptly sacked! Without a phone, I had no way of letting my boss know what had happened. But Mr Bourne was already on the offensive, stating it was outrageous that I hadn't informed them, and gave me a week's notice.

I cried to my Mum when she came over about what had happened, devastated that it was one bad thing after another. She immediately went over to speak to my boss at his office to explain the whole scenario – Dad throwing me out, breaking up with my boyfriend, and then the attack.

I waited outside in reception as Mr Bourne, a quiet man in his fifties, called me in and peered at me through horn-rimmed glasses. Thankfully, he reinstated me with a kind pep talk about letting people know in future what was happening.

The following Saturday, around noon, I headed over to see my friend Eddie for a cuppa and walked past the park. And then, as if it were fate, I shuddered, immediately recognising the ginger-haired man in the playground. He was talking to a few young kids who were playing on the swings. *Shit, it's him, my attacker.*

I raced off to Eddie's place, told him where the man was, and he immediately phoned the police.

Shortly after, the guy was arrested for his assault on me. Evidence was given, statements made, but regardless, he was out on bail straight away whilst waiting for his trial in a month.

I still feared him, but I was relieved knowing the police were on his case and that Ruth, the kind lady upstairs was looking out for me. Getting arrested clearly gave him the shock he needed as he wasn't looking through my window anymore, and I could finally sleep through the night and eat properly again.

When the day in court arrived, I attended with my solicitor in tow. He reassured me that justice would be served and there'd be no need for me to give evidence. Sadly, that wasn't the case. The judge didn't give him a prison sentence, despite him having previous convictions.

I felt angry that someone as dangerous as him wasn't locked away, but at least there was an injunction imposed for him to stay away from me. And I hoped that the legal slap would keep him at bay.

CHAPTER TEN

Help! I Need Somebody

After everything I'd been through, I was feeling very sorry for myself, so I wrote a letter to my old school friend Carolyn saying that I was having difficulty making ends meet and would she like to move in with me.

She wrote back saying she was totally up for it, so we visited her parents in Leckhampton about an hour's walk away, to ask permission.

Carolyn was slim and five foot nothing with long blonde hair and a pale complexion, and her mum was a tiny lady too. She hailed from Wales with curly black hair and an olive complexion and welcomed us in with big hugs. Her dad was equally lovely, tall with kind eyes, his lips always set into a warm smile.

Her parents already knew me from college and over a pot of tea and cake, they agreed that Carolyn could move in. So that was that. My best friend packed up all her things and brought them back to mine. It suited Carolyn too as she was engaged to an army lad who was away for months at a time.

Over the next year, Carolyn and I became inseparable enjoying our independence. We worked hard, played hard and embraced life. Being the late sixties, flower power along with peace and love were a huge part of that era. Respectable secretaries during the week, we discarded our sensible clothes to be weekend hippies dressed in miniskirts and see-through tops, worn braless, along with fashionable knee-high boots.

But I was still hurt and angry about how Bill threw me aside as if I meant nothing. So, when the annual college dance came up, I knew he'd be there. This is my chance, I thought, to see him face to face again, and show him what he's missing.

That evening, Carolyn and I got dressed to kill. I wore a clingy silk dress in crème with sparkly bits. And Carolyn wore a mini dress that was so short if she lifted her arms, everyone would have seen what she'd had for breakfast!

I strutted into the hall on a mission scanning the place for Bill. I soon spotted him by the bar and my stomach flipped over. He looked incredibly handsome as usual wearing an expensive-looking shirt and newly pressed trousers. Then someone nudged him and he and his entourage of six friends all turned and stared at me.

The glamour girl he'd left me for was standing right beside him looking like statuesque perfection. Feeling intimated, I breathlessly made straight for the loos with my head held high. When I glanced back, Bill and his friends were still staring at me, and I thought, *Good, get a load of me, mate.* I wanted him to see how hot I looked, but I was also in a complete state about seeing him again with mad butterflies in my stomach.

Sweeping into the loo with fake confidence, I was faced with three bemused men all turning away from the urinals. Apologetic and blushing, I turned and walked back out. Bill's crowd were now laughing and nudging each other having watched me. I was mortified. I'd accomplished what I'd set out to do, make an entrance, but not in quite the way I hoped. Carolyn grabbed my arm and ushered me into the ladies next door.

Once, I'd calmed down, powdered my nose, and applied another slick of lipstick, we both strode back out. The band started playing Beatles songs, and I began jiving with Carolyn as these two blokes came up and danced along with us.

I secretly hoped that Bill would approach me, and thankfully, he did, striding towards me.

Turning towards him, I stepped away from the others.

"Hi," he said, "Didn't expect to see you here. How are you?"

I was beyond nervous, my hands shaking, but the cider I'd already knocked back gave me a surge of confidence. "Really good, thanks," I lied.

I'd arrived wearing the engagement ring that he'd given me, but now I knew that he and his model girlfriend were still together, I took it off and handed it back not wanting anything that reminded me of him. "Here you are," I said with a smile. I knew if I wanted to move on, and not keep pining for what might have been, I had to remove every piece of him from my life.

"Look," he said gazing into my eyes, "Can we still see each other as friends?"

I laughed as I glanced at his girlfriend by the bar. "Really," I said, "I wonder what Little Miss Perfect would say about that."

For once, he was completely speechless.

CHAPTER ELEVEN

1968 – A Sixties Wild Child

Carolyn was my number one fellow adventurer. We went on so many crazy escapades, making the most of our newfound liberty. One Saturday in the centre of Cheltenham, we were grooving with a crowd of hippies who were paying homage to the summer solstice. It was glorious; we were surrounded by the lush greenery of the park in all its beauty, the sun was out, guitars were strummed, and people sang.

It wasn't long before we met a couple of guys – Dennis, a classically trained guitarist who looked a bit like Jesus with long curly hair. And then there was Ray who wore a moustache and a cheeky grin. Carolyn had her eye on Dennis, and I fancied Ray like mad.

I was dancing barefoot along with everyone else wearing my normal hippy garb – a flowing dress, bangles, and beads, with flowers in my floppy hat. Unfortunately, my picture was snapped by a photographer in all my bohemian glory, and I appeared on the front page of the local newspaper the next day. That did not bode well for me. My boss who was very old school was shocked and called me in.

"I wouldn't expect one of my secretaries to publically dress like this," he snapped.

I knew he'd already given me a second chance, so, I decided to look for another job rather than waiting to get sacked.

Soon after, Carolyn and I both got jobs as Visual Display Unit (VDU) operators at Eagle Star Insurance Company which was only a five-minute walk away. We were riding high. We split the bills, both earning six pounds, five shillings a week and worked nine to five, Monday to Friday. Our weekends were spent relaxing in Cheltenham Beer Gardens in Imperial Square mingling with other like-minded hippies along with our new boyfriends, Dennis and Ray, imbibing whatever was our particular high. On other weekends, Car and I enjoyed trips to Wales in her Ford Anglia, spending uncomfortable nights sleeping in the car.

Before long, the bedsit became too cramped for the two of us, so Carolyn and I moved into a bigger studio nearby on Bath Road. We were both beyond excited as it had a larger bedroom and was self-contained, so we wouldn't have to share our bathroom with strangers anymore.

Our new pad soon became the fashionable place to be, even though it was tiny. "Come over at the weekend and hang out," we'd say to all our friends and acquaintances. And people just drifted in and out, day and night. There was barely any food in the house or anything worth stealing so it didn't concern us. We even had a regular D.J. who played the Beatles, the Beach Boys, and Simon and Garfunkel. He had a crazy sense of humour, keeping us laughing and on a constant high.

I still remember vividly when Dennis and Ray came over. It was a rite of passage when they gave us our first joint. We all sat crossed-legged on the bed as I took a few puffs, spluttering and wheezing.

"Take it into your lungs," Dennis said, showing me how as he pulled on his spliff.

So, I did. And being a novice, I promptly passed out!

I came round feeling dizzy a few moments later and was sick on the floor. The next thing I knew I was being cleaned up and put to bed by Carolyn. However, with practice, I soon got used to inhaling weed.

Those liberating times freed our spirits as well as loosened our morals. The pill had only just been legalised in 1967 for all women rather than just those who were married. And in 1968, the Women's Liberation Movement came into being which sought equal rights and opportunities for women. It felt as if we were part of our own feminist movement, supporting ourselves, sleeping with any man that took our fancy, and paying our own way. So that little tablet became a necessity.

However, it became tricky trying to hide our antics from our respective mothers. My mum would arrive by coach every Saturday, spend the day with us, and then leave on the 4.00 p.m. bus, so we'd plan not to have anyone there at the time. But Carolyn's mum, nicknamed 'Gee' would pop in at any given moment.

On one occasion of many, we heard Gee's voice echoing up the stairs. "Hello. Anyone home? It's only me."

As I heard Gee walk upstairs, Carolyn ran into the hallway and yanked her mother into the kitchen, so I had time to get rid of Ray.

"Quick, hurry," I whispered as he grabbed his clothes, scrambled out of the room naked, and raced downstairs.

Another time, when Gee spontaneously popped in, we pushed Dennis, Carolyn's naked boyfriend, into the large walk-in cupboard at the top of the stairs, his clothes flung in after him. He emerged after Gee finally left, looking like a vagrant who'd wandered in from the street. It was certainly a time of laughter, joy, and fun.

A New-Found Haven

Carolyn and I continued to live like decadent mad things, but after a year, our bedsit felt more like a drop-in centre. It became draining to constantly find people sitting on our bed strumming a guitar or helping themselves to our food and leaving a mess. And someone was always in the bathroom when we needed the loo. So, we found a one-bedroom cottage called 'Here-we-are' which was halfway up Leckhampton Hill – a rural haven that became Carolyn's home for the next thirty-five years.

Finally, we had a living room with a fireplace as well as spring water that fed into a tank. There was also an outside loo in the garage where you chucked down a bucket of water to flush it, but we didn't mind, we were in our element enjoying the beauty of our surroundings where you could see the outline of Cheltenham in the valley amidst rolling hills dotted with cows, sheep and goats.

My boyfriend, Ray, moved in as well as Carolyn's boyfriend, Dennis, the classical guitarist. All four of us could have been a cosy little family unit, but unfortunately, as the months rolled on, things went downhill.

Whilst Carolyn and I were at work all day, the two unemployed boys hung around the cottage. I later discovered that Ray was dealing in amphetamines and his 'clients' were constantly popping in and out. Understandably, Carolyn was fed up with coming home to dirty dishes in the sink and empty cupboards.

We plodded on for a year with a rather tense atmosphere until one morning over breakfast Carolyn and Dennis announced they were getting married. It was then suggested that Ray and I needed to find another home. That was her 'nice' way of getting rid of us.

I took the hint, not wanting to disrupt my friend's life any further, so Ray and I packed up our things, not knowing where we were going to live.

Initially, we moved in with Ray's parents in Cheltenham, sleeping in the front room of their B & B on a sofa bed. But being back with parents always meant strict ground rules, so we quickly rented a first-floor bedsit in a Victorian townhouse which had a shared bathroom in the hallway. A couple of friendly Hell's Angels were in a room on the same floor.

Everything seemed fine, except our new landlord, Mr Thompson, took some getting used to. He was a schoolmaster at Cheltenham Boys College and resided on the ground floor with his wife. And we soon discovered that they were both naturists!

In the morning, I'd come downstairs to head off to work and he'd call out "Morning Mary." I'd turn round to find him walking around in his birthday suit with a smirk on his face. I'd blush and feel extremely awkward.

Thankfully, I had a female ally to chat to amongst all these men – a single mum called Sue who lived in the basement with her three-year-old son. Sue and I became good friends and when Carolyn was due to marry Dennis in Leckhampton church, I had nothing suitable to wear, so she lent me a purple mini dress and a floppy hat. Then she curled my hair and put make-up on me including false eyelashes. I stared at myself in the mirror afterwards and thought, *Wow, Twiggy, eat your heart out.*

Soon after, Ray came downstairs to say we had to leave for the wedding until suddenly, we heard shouting. All three of us glanced at each other anxiously wondering what on earth was going on, and then we crept upstairs, totally unprepared for the greeting.

Our landlord, Mr Thompson, came out of his kitchen, fully clothed for once, brandishing a shotgun and shouting, his face red and contorted. "I'll kill you both, you little assholes, using my house like a railway station."

I honestly thought he was going to shoot us. We had to get to the wedding but in a panic Ray and I ran back to the safety of our room, locking the door as Sue raced back down to her basement flat. I knew Carolyn would wonder where we were, but what could we do, we were stuck in that damned room, too terrified to come out whilst Thompson was still off his head yelling.

Forty-five minutes later, the Hells Angels guys became our saviours. Wearing the traditional black leather with the eagle on the back of their jackets, they arrived to discover Mr Thompson pacing the floor with a shotgun and called the police.

Once the cops turned up, we hoped our crazy landlord would be arrested. Unfortunately, no charges were made as he had a firearms certificate, and the gun was being used on his premises, so it wasn't an arrestable offence! That meant he could continue to aggressively bully us. But we used the opportunity amidst all the chaos to rush out of the front door, making it to Carolyn's wedding just in time to see her and her new husband coming out of the arched doorway of the church with confetti falling over them.

After the wedding reception, we knew we had to get away from that unhinged nutcase and hurried back to collect our possessions. After another quick stint at Ray's parent's place, I found us yet another bedsit, and sadly, my life sank into an even bigger black hole.

In terms of earning a wage, I was now a receptionist for a car dealership, but I was beginning to see that Ray was a complete waster. I'd turned into chief, cook and bottle washer with sex thrown in, cleaning up after his skanky clients, taking washing to the laundrette, and cooking all our meals whilst he kept promising that a job was on the horizon. The truth was, he was more interested in easy money from drug dealing so he could continue to laze around.

Why did I continue to tolerate him you might ask? Well, back then, I hated being alone where my fears and insecurities were magnified. I was also smoking a lot of dope and barely eating, so the weight dropped off me. I wouldn't even let my mum visit because I was so embarrassed by the scrawny waif I'd turned into. So as sad as it might sound, I felt vulnerable and needed someone, even a scrounger like him.

By the end of the summer, life took on an all-time low. Ray's dope and amphetamine business was booming, and I'd come home to find endless strangers in the house. I was frail and miserable as he constantly criticised me, saying, "You're no oil painting, are you?" or "You're too skinny."

Then one morning, I was standing in the hallway and overheard my new landlord talking to the milkman. "It's such a shame. That chick has a lot going for her but she's wasting it all on a no-good parasite."

I stood still for a moment, gobsmacked. *Oh god, they're talking about me!* I was twenty years old and falling apart. I didn't want to be seen as a victim or the subject of gossip, but I realised, somehow, I've got to get rid of this idiot.

I'd lost contact with Carolyn and Dennis up at the cottage with our mutual busy lives, but a few days later, Carolyn, turned up. I burst into tears when I saw her on the doorstep. She told me that the milkman who delivered to us was actually her brother. He'd recognised me from seeing me at Carolyn's wedding and was deeply worried. What a coincidence! An angel must have been looking out for me.

When Carolyn and I talked, she made me take a long hard look at myself. Sitting down on a kitchen chair, she pulled out some photos from her handbag. "Oh, Mary, sweetheart, you're gorgeous in these wedding photos but look at you now. What's happened? You look like a Biafran."

I explained my situation with Ray and that I didn't know how to get out of it.

"I don't have all the answers, but I'm always here when you need me," she said touching my hand. "Keep strong and keep in touch. We can meet for coffee."

Her words were a lifeline to me. Sometimes all we need in times of struggle is for someone to show that they care. And I knew, that somehow, I had to turn my life around. But how?

1952 - Me as a baby in the prefab home

*At my first communion, age 10,
with brother Pat, 13*

My parents' Audrey and James with me and Pat

1966 - me age 15 on the far right, escaping to my friend,
Tessa's parent's dairy farm in Bourton-on-the-Water

Me on the tractor at the dairy farm

Me and Tessa, age 15

Relaxing after school in Bourton-on-the-Water

Me on the far right with schoolfriends
dressed in the sixties fashion

Me aged 15

*1968 - Passing my driving test for the first time
in fiance Bill's van*

Picnic with Bill's dog Tansy in a field near home

1969 - age 18. Me at Carolyn's wedding to Dennis.
The day of the shotgun!

Carolyn's cottage 'Here-we-are' - the middle cottage halfway up Leckhampton Hill, Cheltenham

Motorcycle racing champion, Dave Browning

A gorgeous Dave, before the accident

*1973 - Albuquerque, New Mexico. Me pictured with
Chris's girlfriend, Jooles in the camper van.*

1974 - My brother, Pat with Dave taken at Pat's Wedding to Jean in Appleby, Cumbria

1974, age 23 with the sporty MGB that Dave got me

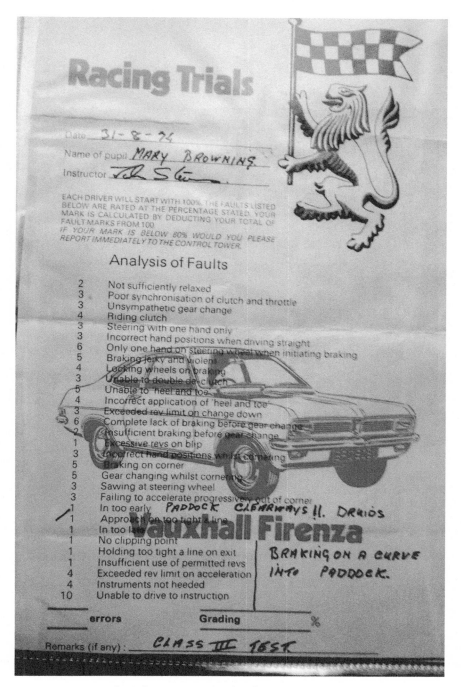

Racing Trials

Date 31-8-74

Name of pupil MARY BROWNING

Instructor John Stewart

EACH DRIVER WILL START WITH 100%. THE FAULTS LISTED BELOW ARE RATED AT THE PERCENTAGE STATED. YOUR MARK IS CALCULATED BY DEDUCTING YOUR TOTAL OF FAULT MARKS FROM 100.
IF YOUR MARK IS BELOW 60% WOULD YOU PLEASE REPORT IMMEDIATELY TO THE CONTROL TOWER.

Analysis of Faults

2	Not sufficiently relaxed
3	Poor synchronisation of clutch and throttle
3	Unsympathetic gear change
4	Riding clutch
3	Steering with one hand only
3	Incorrect hand positions when driving straight
6	Only one hand on steering wheel when initiating braking
5	Braking jerky and violent
4	Locking wheels on braking
3	Unable to double de-clutch
5	Unable to 'heel and toe'
4	Incorrect application of 'heel and toe'
3	Exceeded rev limit on change down
6	Complete lack of braking before gear change
2	Insufficient braking before gear change
1	Excessive revs on blip
3	Incorrect hand positions whilst cornering
5	Braking on corner
5	Gear changing whilst cornering
3	Sawing at steering wheel
3	Failing to accelerate progressively out of corner
1	In too early PADDOCK. CLEARWAYS II. DRUIDS
1	Approach too tight a line
1	In too late
1	No clipping point
1	Holding too tight a line on exit
1	Insufficient use of permitted revs
4	Exceeded rev limit on acceleration
4	Instruments not heeded
10	Unable to drive to instruction

BRAKING ON A CURVE INTO PADDOCK.

errors _____   Grading _____   %

Remarks (if any): CLASS III TEST

1974 - The Racing Trial info to win a racing car

1974 - Winning the racing car with SHE Magazine

1975 - My wedding to Dave after the accident. I was 24. Pictured with my mum and dad, Dave's Dad Jack with his new partner, Carol, and Carol's daughter, Louisa, who was my Bridesmaid.

Another wedding photo of me and Dave.
His sister, Lynn, is on the far left

My 'antique' shop, Reflections on Cheltenham High Street

1978 - Carolyn's wedding to Colin. Dave back to good health.
Me with Carolyn's dog, Tumbleweed.

1978 - Me at Carolyn's wedding, age, 27

1982 - Meeting my second husband, Jim, in Ibiza

1989 - Getting married to Jim

1989 - My witness Helen and friend Mo at my wedding to Jim

Wedding celebrations at The Bricklayers Arms,
Central London which Jim and I managed

*Mike, the wonderful acupuncturist and his equally
amazing partner, Maggie*

PART 3

DAVE

Get your motor runnin'
Head out on the highway
Looking for adventure
In whatever comes our way
Born to Be Wild

CHAPTER TWELVE

1971 – Love is in the Air

It was Christmas Eve and whilst working at my job at VW motors, a mechanic called Pash asked me out for a drink. For the record, he wasn't my type – five foot two and stocky, plus he had a girlfriend and a kid. But I was depressed, and he treated me like a lady and made me laugh, so I eventually accepted his invitation to go to a Xmas party at the local pub.

Ray had disappeared again, as he often did for days at a time. I presumed he'd gone to his parents for the holidays, or he'd be scrounging drinks somewhere, telling everyone he was a roadie for Black Sabbath. But frankly, I was passed caring.

After work, I got togged up in my best gear – hot pants and my 'lady white boots' and skipped along to the pub with an overnight bag as mum wanted me home for Christmas with or without Dad's consent.

As soon as we walked into the pub, I saw a guy sitting at the bar with a little boy perched on his knee and thought, *That's a dish and a half.* He had these bright blue Paul Newman eyes and a thick mop of chestnut hair. And he was dressed stylishly wearing a leather jacket and bell bottom trousers we used to call 'Loons.'

Pash introduced us as they were friends who worked in the motor trade, and I discovered that his name was Dave Browning. Like a lovesick schoolgirl, I couldn't stop staring and smiling at him – there was a vibe between us, an electricity that I couldn't explain.

I started playing darts with Pash when a lady came in with a tray full of handmade gollywogs. Being a lover of anything handmade, I asked Pash to buy one. He ignored me and carried on playing darts. Then the dishy guy, Dave, called the lady over to the bar and bought one, which I assumed, was for his son.

An hour later, as we left the pub, Dave came up to me and Pash, and I could finally see how tall he was. He must have been around six-foot-two.

"Have a wonderful Christmas," he said, looking down at me. He then handed me the beautiful gollywog and before I knew it, he gave me a sneaky kiss under the mistletoe hanging over the front door. "Happy Christmas," he said, again, and then quickly disappeared into the night with his kid.

I was elated, my stomach flipping over. *Oh my God, he kissed me and bought me the gollywog.* I felt so special. They were innocent stuffed toys back then and not loaded with the PC connotations of today.

When Pash drove me to the bus station, I told him that I fancied his friend.

"Don't go there," he said, narrowing his eyes. "He's twenty-six, anyway, so far too old for you. And he's a womaniser. He's had loads of kids with different women."

I don't care, I thought, *he's gorgeous.*

But that kiss ignited something in me, and in the days that followed, I couldn't stop thinking about Dave, unable to eat, sleep or think straight. So, after the Xmas holidays, I turned into Inspector Clouseau, searching out places that this gorgeous guy would frequent.

It seemed like fate when a few weeks later, we bumped into one another outside a club on the promenade. Our eyes met and there was that crazy chemistry again. I immediately said yes when he asked if he could drop me home and tried not to look too shocked when he opened the door of his sapphire-blue E-Type Jag!

"Fancy coming back to mine for a drink?" he asked.

I gave him a huge grin and nodded. The last thing I wanted to do was go back to Ray or an empty place. So off we headed to his attic apartment in a select part of town.

When I walked in, I was shocked. It was so different from my slum of a place —everything was tidy and smelt clean. We relaxed in the living area on the sofa and listened to Led Zeppelin and Pink Floyd, enjoying a joint. I didn't ask any prying questions about his so-called womanising. I knew Pash was after me and would say anything to put me off, so I decided to wait for Dave to tell me about his life. Eventually, he did give away snippets about himself – he had two sons aged two and five who he picked up once a week from their mother's. I wasn't remotely broody, but they were part of him, so I hoped I'd meet them at some point.

It must have been around 2 a.m. when I got up to leave, and he asked if he could walk me home. I said, no, despite it being late. I explained that I wasn't happy in my relationship and was worried Ray might see him and cause a scene.

"Well, if you ever want breathing space, you're welcome to crash at mine!" he said with a twinkle in his eyes.

When I got home, Ray was standing in the kitchen area with his arms folded and a scowl on his face. "Where have you been?" he snapped.

I ignored him as he blathered on and on. He was livid that doormat Mary wasn't at his beck and call anymore. But I was determined to keep my new love interest a secret. He wasn't going to ruin my dreams again.

One evening, a few days later, sick of my miserable life, I plucked up the courage and knocked on Dave's door. He welcomed me in, and we again smoked a joint, listened to music and drank whisky. Getting to know each other as friends continued for a few weeks until the day came when we finally slept together.

Dave had his own company repairing and selling second-hand cars, and the following day he rang me at work and said he needed to see me urgently, in person. *Oh! shit of all shits.* My stomach was churning with a feeling of impending doom. He'd finally bedded me, and now he wanted to dump me, I told myself as my self-worth plummeted. After all, what would a handsome guy like him want with me as his girlfriend anyway? He could have anyone he desired.

We met at his flat and as we sat down at the kitchen table opposite each other, he said with a concerned voice, "Babe, I don't know how to tell you this …"

He hesitated as I stared at him, worried sick. "What's wrong," I mumbled.

"I've got crabs," he blurted out.

I couldn't help but grin. *Phew!* That was a thank the lord moment. It might sound disgusting, but at the time, I was more relieved he wasn't dumping me.

He rang his mum, and she sorted out a potion from the chemist and told him to inform anyone else he'd slept with to get some too. Dave still wanted me around his apartment as the casual girlfriend, but

Pash was right – my guy was obviously going with all sorts. As weak as it might sound, after having my confidence annihilated by Ray, I was thrilled that he even considered me.

Thankfully, soon after, Dave appeared to have a change of tune about his lothario lifestyle and asked me to move in. I was thrilled, packing up my belongings that very day, feeling like the chosen one from a long line of women. He even had a nickname for me: 'Doodles' after my surname Doody. That was a sure sign of affection in my eyes.

My new beau was keen for me to meet his parents, so he booked a table at the posh Queen's hotel, one of the biggest five-star hotels in Cheltenham – all white tablecloths, crystal glasses and steel cutlery. I was nervous having never been to a posh dinner before and didn't know what order to use the cutlery in. I also prayed that his parents would like me.

Dave's mother, Joyce was sitting on a stool by the bar for pre-dinner drinks whilst his father, Jack, stood beside her. I'd heard that she worked in a fashionable boutique, and you could tell. She looked young for her forty-something years, her slim figure encased in a tailored blue skirt suit. Dave's dad was equally smart in a black suit and tie. He owned a second-hand car dealership and was tall and tanned with black curly hair. I went to shake his mum's hand and she leaned in and hugged me which took me by surprise. I knew then that she must be a warm, caring lady.

After dinner, we headed to a motor racing club where Dave and his father were members, and I soon had the shock of my life. As we entered the place, I saw numerous pictures of Dave on the wall. He was holding some trophies.

"What happened there? Did you win something?" I asked Dave innocently as we stood by the snack bar.

"Oh, he won something all right," said his father with a chuckle as he went on to tell me that Dave was a motorcycle racing driver who'd won the 1969 British Championship. "He raced at Brands Hatch, Silverstone, and Mallory Park to name a few and won two silver replicas in the 1970 and 1971 Isle of Man TT races (aka Tourist Trophy Races)," his dad continued. "He also took part in several European Grands Prix including Holland, Spain, Germany, Belgium, Ulster as well as the U.S.A."

"Wow, that sounds amazing. Why didn't you tell me?" I asked Dave, my eyes shining with excitement.

Dave slouched over and flushed red. A lot of guys would crow about their success, but he was always very humble and just shrugged his shoulders. "That's all in the past," he replied.

"But why did you retire when you were doing so well?"

"That bad boy, Barry Sheen arrived on the racing scene," his father interjected, "and Dave didn't feel he could compete." He looked sideways at Dave. "Isn't that right, son?"

"More or less," answered Dave as he grabbed my hand to introduce me to some motorcyclists that had just arrived.

Later that evening, when we got back to his place, Dave told me that his mum had asked him: "Are you going to keep this one? We really like her."

I was so happy. It's amazing how my whole life had turned around from being with a waster like Ray who criticised me constantly. I was like a flower in the sunshine around Dave. It's almost as if he could see my potential as he complimented me daily, telling me I was clever and beautiful. My confidence soared as I made more of myself, wearing tight jeans, miniskirts, and hot pants. Although it took me a while to get used to the upmarket lifestyle where we had a weekly cleaner, I also had money to spend and was regularly treated to dinner and the cinema.

Unfortunately, my selfish ex must have followed me to my new home at some point as one evening he banged on Dave's front door, crying and creating a scene. I knew it was him outside and ignored him. But after this went on for a week, Dave rolled his eyes and said that I'd better go and deal with it.

I stomped downstairs, opened the door, and said sharply, "Get lost, Ray. You've lost your meal ticket."

He stared back at me with watery eyes and eventually walked off sheepishly into the night, and I felt a surge of newfound strength for speaking my truth and confronting him face to face.

When Dave came home from work, he handed me some keys. "It's not much but it will get you about until something better comes into the garage."

I rushed outside with him to take a look, my eyes shining – my very own car, an old Ford estate. I was now Miss Independent. I could drive to and from work and pick mum up on a Saturday from the bus station when she visited.

My relationship with Dave was an exciting whirlwind. I'd never flown on an aeroplane before and only went overseas once, on a school trip to Germany by ship. Suddenly we were on holiday in Alicante for a week in a plush hotel with views over the mountains. We hired a car and went sightseeing, and headed to the beach by day, and the restaurants and bars by night. We fell passionately, madly, wildly in love, cuddling and holding hands all the time, not wanting to spend a second apart.

I changed my job yet again. It was so easy in those days, so I became an express delivery driver for a motor trader in Cheltenham and the surrounding villages, delivering exhausts, batteries, and engine parts.

Dave thought it was a great idea. By traditional standards, it wasn't the typical job for a girl, but I loved driving and got bored easily, so this would mean I was out and about, meeting people. And I had the freedom to drop in and see Dave in the garage.

It wasn't long before I met the missing puzzle piece from Dave's family – his sister, Lynn. She often popped into the garage as her husband, Merv, worked there with Dave as a mechanic. But despite looking glam with bleached blonde hair and a shapely figure, Dave told me she had mental health problems.

From a young age, she'd repeatedly tried to commit suicide, slashing her wrists or overdosing. The entire family were always on a knife edge and tried everything to make her happy, even going so far as to buy her breast implants. Eventually, she was put on antipsychotics and sectioned in Coney Hill, a mental health institution in Gloucester. She was there for weeks receiving electric shock treatment.

Dave was an easy-going guy and nothing much fazed him, but the way he talked about Lynne told me he was worried sick. I grew closer with his family often going out for dinner with them all, until his mother said to me in front of everyone, "I wonder if you'd consider being a part-time companion to Lynn as you get on so well."

I glanced at Lynne and smiled as she smiled back. "I'd love to," I replied, and soon I was taking her out every week for a coffee or some shopping. They all knew she was safe with me, and she was happy because she didn't have any other friends.

CHAPTER THIRTEEN

1972 – Betrayal and Despair

Out of the blue, Dave's mum, Joyce, rang him in a state of shock. "Jack has jetted off to Spain with a woman twenty years younger."

"What the hell," said Dave in shock.

The woman's name was Carol and she had two young children. All his father left behind was a note saying: *Sorry, but I want to start a new life!*

Dave blamed himself for not nipping things in the bud. He had an inkling something was happening between his father and this Carol woman. Apparently, she kept calling into the garage with her car and being flirty with Jack, making lots of eye contact.

I was gobsmacked. Compared to my dysfunctional upbringing with my drunken father, I thought the Brownings were the perfect family.

Dave and I knew that Joyce would be devastated, reeling from the betrayal that she never saw coming, so we both moved in with her for a few nights. We all convened in the living room, the house eerily quiet without his talkative dad around. Dave sat beside his mum with his arm around her trying to give her some kind of comfort.

A few hours later, Dave and I drove over to tell his sister, Lynne, as his mother was still too distraught. She lived in a little village just outside Cheltenham, but it wasn't good timing – she was just out of Coney Hill and coping as well as she could – but she fell to pieces when she heard the news, sobbing and spluttering, trying to catch her breath. "How could he do this to us?" she said as she slumped on the sofa wiping her tears away with a tissue.

Merv, her husband was so concerned, he gave her some tranquillisers to try and calm her down, and then sat beside her, holding her hands, his face pale. He really was her rock, but she was in such a state, we were worried about her being sectioned again.

We headed back to Joyce's, and by the third day, she appeared to have made a miraculous recovery. She popped out to get her hair done, bought a new outfit, and then told us when she got back that we could go home. "I'm coping now, thanks, lovies. I'm going back to work in the boutique tomorrow morning."

Dave and I were relieved she was feeling more like her old self, but still concerned, we called in on her at work the following afternoon to double-check.

When we walked in, she seemed perfectly cheery, chatting with her colleagues. Dave followed up by phoning her in the evening, and she again sounded happy, telling us she'd had a good day but was tired and heading off to bed.

Unbeknownst to us, in the early hours of the morning, that same night, Joyce drove to the middle of a wood, downed an entire bottle of sleeping pills, washed down with her favourite Gin, and killed herself!

As you can imagine, nothing prepared any of us for this. The police came to the garage, and when they told Dave the heartbreaking news, he just stood there gaping at them in horror. I never saw him cry, not then, or in the weeks to come, but his body language told a different story, the way he shook his head and shrugged his shoulders in disbelief. The poor guy was traumatised, and I was devastated that his mother had acted so impulsively without leaving a note to give us an idea of how she was feeling. It certainly seemed that fragile mental health ran in the family.

That evening, within a week of his father leaving, Dave drove us once again to Lynne's house to deliver more traumatic news. We dreaded her reaction knowing how fragile she was, but we couldn't hide the truth from her.

Dave sat beside her holding her hands in his and swallowing hard. "Sis, something awful has happened. Mum's committed suicide. They found her body in the woods."

I wasn't sure if Lynne had properly digested his words, but she just sat there silently, staring into the distance. Then she got up and paced the room, gulping in air. I didn't know what to do for the best, so I went into the kitchen and switched on the kettle to make tea. Merv, her childhood sweetheart, walked over and wrapped his arm around her as he'd done before. "I'm here for you, darling," he whispered. But I wasn't sure how much more tragedy the poor girl could take.

Dave phoned his father in Spain that night and he got on a flight back to the UK the next day. After Jack arrived back at his former marital home, we went over there to discuss the funeral arrangements. Sitting around the dining table, Dave blurted out, "You realise you've killed Mum by leaving her. I'll never forgive you for that."

Jack was speechless, clenching his hands, his face pale. He had nothing to say because he knew he was guilty and couldn't deny it.

Joyce's funeral was held in a church in Cheltenham where she was buried in the cemetery grounds. During the service, Jack stood there sheepishly with his head hanging down not wanting to make eye contact with anyone. And I knew that despite his stoic appearance, Dave felt an enormous pressure to balance his grief for his mother with attempting to keep his sister safe and alive.

A few days after, just as I thought, Lynn was sectioned again for her own safety. Once more burdened by grief, she'd attempted another overdose and tried to drive her car off a motorway bridge. Somehow, she survived.

I visited her at Coney Hill twice a week trying to offer some positivity, support and comfort. Meanwhile, Jack didn't hang around. Within six months, he'd sold the family home, went back to Spain, and married his mistress, Carol. Before he left, he gave Dave a fifty per cent share in the garage, J.B. Autos, to keep it going.

I was also busy with Dave's two boys, taking on the role of surrogate mother every other weekend. I hadn't met their mum at the time as Dave would always collect seven-year-old Mark and five-year-old Peter and bring them to our place. The two of them were always bursting with energy, so we'd take them for long country walks to wear them out, and they wolfed down everything that was put in front of them.

A few months later, Jack was back in the UK and bought another house in Cheltenham with his new wife and two stepchildren.

Dave was still nursing a lot of anger towards his father. You could see it in his eyes whenever he looked at him as if a fire had been lit. Once again, I became the peacemaker and negotiator, just as I had in my childhood as a go-between to my parents. I talked to Dave and then his father, trying to smooth things over as Dave refused to speak to him. "Your dad has invited us over for a family dinner to meet his new wife," I said one evening over a plate of lasagne. "He *really* wants to see you."

Dave took a mouthful of food and then snapped, "I don't want to meet that tart or her brats."

But somehow, I persuaded him. "Don't you think there's been enough loss and heartbreak already without bearing a grudge?"

He finally nodded in agreement. "Okay," he answered, "but I'm not staying long."

Lynne had also been invited but declined. She hadn't met Carol and the way she saw it, this slut had stormed into their lives, stolen their father, and murdered their mother.

Unsurprisingly, dinner was a stilted affair as we tucked into a Chile Con Carne and a bottle of Rioja with me and Carol making most of the conversation. She was a looker though that's for sure – five foot seven with an hourglass figure, she had a Mediterranean vibe with her thick, coffee-coloured hair and dark brown eyes. But by the end of the awkward evening, I was glad to go home.

We all needed some positive news after all the sadness, and it was soon after her mother's death that Lynne finally fell pregnant after seven years of trying to conceive. She and Merv came over to tell us their news as they walked in holding hands. And Dave and I hoped that by focusing on this longed-for baby, it would help alleviate her suicidal thoughts.

CHAPTER FOURTEEN

1973 – Spanish Chaos

After living together for two years, Dave wanted to escape all the trauma and misery, so we moved to a two-bed flat in the Cotswold village of Painswick, twenty miles away, to be around the healing energy of the countryside.

I adored our new place. The flat was a converted dairy set on a hill with scenic views over lush green meadows. A pet hedgehog came with the place, and we agreed with the landlord that we'd look after him, feeding him lettuce. There was a bakery next door and local shops nearby, and the village also had the most beautiful church, famous for having ninety-nine yew trees on the grounds. The rumour was that when they planted another one to make it one hundred, one yew tree would always die.

I knew Dave was still grieving, but he seemed angry about everything, powerless in his frustration to make things better. I was so tuned into him that even without him saying a word, I was well aware of the hurt he was feeling because of the upbringing I'd had. In many ways, it helped me empathise. I'd hug him often, and say, "Dave, I'm here for you as long as you want me."

Despite his grief, he was still a wonderful partner to me, spoiling me and boosting my confidence. And in March, Dave and I were off to Alicante again, only this time staying at his father's apartment. Jack had offered the trip as a birthday pressie to me but also asked Dave to pick up an old minivan he'd left behind that urgently needed moving, otherwise, it would be towed away.

We didn't mind as his dad was paying, so the plan was to spend a week there sunbathing and then drive the van fourteen hundred miles back to Painswick.

However, once we got there, Dave was horrified by the state of the van – it was a rusty old wreck that made a strange chugging noise when he started driving it. Then the fan belt broke in the middle of the night somewhere in Andorra. I had to take off my tights so they could be used as a substitute. And when we reached the road to Bilbao aiming to catch the next ferry, we were stopped by police. The road was blocked off because of snow and the cops said we should turn back.

But no, not stubborn old Dave. "Don't be silly," he said, "We've come this far. We want to get home so we're not going back."

"Continue at your own risk, then," said a policeman raising an eyebrow as if he thought Dave was nuts.

I admit I was nervous about Dave's decision. With all the snow, hail, and freezing temperatures, I had to keep getting out to clean the windscreen as the wipers wouldn't work.

Eventually arriving in Bilbao with the exhaust clanging, the van held together with no more than tights and rope, we found a hotel to kip in, close to the ferry.

The next morning, Dave started the engine up, and bang, the exhaust fell off. Trundling down to the harbour with the van making a right racket, we were stopped by police again. I thought after our nightmare ordeal, they wouldn't let us on the ferry, but after hearing of our epic journey, the cops seemed sympathetic and escorted us onto the boat. I bet they were glad to see the rear end of the van disappearing into the lower deck.

When we finally arrived in Southampton, the blimmin' van wouldn't start, so it had to be pushed off the ferry by Dave and members of the crew. As you can imagine after twenty hours on the road, we were exhausted. So much for my wonderful birthday break in Spain.

Dave was livid with his dad. "Cheers," he said when he took the broken vehicle to the garage, "I hope you're proud of yourself for putting our lives in danger."

His dad just shrugged his shoulders and smirked.

I like to be in America

That same year, Dave whisked me overseas again when we spent the entire month of October in Albuquerque, New Mexico with his friends, Chris, and his girlfriend Jooles. They were both Brits – Chris was tall, lean and blond, and worked as a jaguar mechanic. His company had sent him to the US office because of his expertise. Jooles was slight with long brown hair, and she rarely smiled which made it hard to read her.

We were all up for some adventure, so Chris took a month's holiday and the four of us went off in their VW camper van to explore Nevada, taking a tent with us for camping later. And wow, it was a mind-blowing experience for a girl who'd barely travelled. We headed to places like The Petrified Forest where the trees had all fallen, and over the centuries, had turned into multicoloured stones of pink, orange, and brown hues. It was somehow mystical and magical, reminding me of something out of Narnia when the ice queen uses her dark magic to turn things to stone.

Then there was the Grand Canyon which took my breath away. One of the seven wonders of the world and I'm not surprised. Eighteen miles at its widest and a mile deep. I remember all four of us stood on the edge and looked down into the vast cavernous space, and there was an awe-struck silence. What can you say when faced with such beauty?

Our next pit stop was to meet the Zuni Indian Tribe in Nevada. I'd just finished reading a fascinating book called *Bury my Heart at Wounded Knee*, which delved into the history of The American Indians, so I told Dave I was keen to explore their way of life. They're fascinating people with religious beliefs centred on the guidance from ancient ancestors as well as worshipping their deities: Earth Mother, Sun Father, and Moonlight-Giving Mother.

The tribe resided in a small village full of tepees located on a field where the government allowed them to stay. We met with a chief, his wife and their two children who earned their living making souvenirs for tourists such as silver jewellery, moccasins, dream catchers and Indian headdresses. As I mentioned earlier, I love handmade things and Dave bought me a silver bracelet which was embedded with turquoise and amber stones.

During our trip, I warmed up to Jooles a tiny bit more. In fact, the trip solidified more of a stronger friendship between all of us. We then returned to their condo for a few days before flying back to the UK.

CHAPTER FIFTEEN

1974 – Get Ready for Penelope Pitstop

Nine months later in July, I caught sight of *SHE* magazine on the shelf in the newsagents where I now worked. Emblazoned on the front cover were the words: *COMPETITION TO WIN A FORMULA FORD RACING CAR.*

Instantly, I was intrigued, paid for the mag, and rushed home with it after work to read it more thoroughly. The goal was to find a female racing driver as there weren't any at that time. If you won, the car came with a trailer to tow it, a Bell Star fireproof boilersuit, and twenty-five lessons at Brands Hatch along with sponsorship from Brooke-Bond which meant you'd win enough free coffee and tea for a year!

I'd never considered racing before, but I loved driving fast and the sense of freedom it gave me, so why the hell not? There was an extensive questionnaire to see if you had a broad sense of the racing industry as well as good driving abilities, but in all honesty, I was clueless. Fortunately, I had an expert on tap. Dave had triumphed on the motorcycle circuit, so I figured with his expertise, I might just be able to fake it till I made it.

When I showed Dave the magazine, he was as excited as I was, and said, "Go for it. I'll help you all I can."

The new goal was great for both of us, giving us both something positive to focus on, and Dave took it seriously. He stuck maps of Brands Hatch onto the living room walls and either side of the stairs and would quiz me daily on flags, racing terms, and the names of the bends and corners. I posted the application just in time for the competition deadline which was July 31st.

Dave was one of the few people I knew that had a house phone, which was fortunate, as a few weeks later, someone from the mag rang to say I was through to the next stage of the competition— one of a hundred girls who'd been selected from over a thousand. It sounded amazing until they said I'd be invited to the motor racing stables at Brands Hatch, so I could showcase my skills and knowledge, along with the ninety-nine other girls! Ninety-nine other girls! How on earth could I compete with so many chicks and get anywhere?

Either way, I was beyond excited when Dave and I were invited to the racing track on August 31st where I took a written test in one of their offices based on all the racing lingo Dave had coached me in. Then I got into a Vauxhall Firenza for a test drive to see how I handled the car. An instructor sat beside me taking notes on how well I went round the circuit. After we finished, I felt I'd done okay, except for heading into a corner too early, and not accelerating fast enough out of it, but I hoped that wouldn't go against me.

A month later, I discovered I was in the final with twenty-five other girls. Wow. I couldn't believe it. Now, all I had to do was wait patiently for the next letter from them with an update. Whoopee do. Although, I didn't want to get my hopes up too much.

As a double bonus, Dave had more confidence in my driving and let me use his Jag now and then. I felt like a superstar behind the wheel of an expensive car and kept offering to escort friends on shopping trips or simply cruise around town just so I could show off with the roof down. Then Dave got me a little open-top sports car – an MGB Roadster from the garage. He really did spoil me rotten.

In September of that same year, I was invited once more to Brands Hatch. Excitement was mounting. It was close to the bone as now it was just me and two other finalists. Dave's tuition was spot on – I got ninety-eight per cent in the written exam.

With a belly full of butterflies, Dave and I went with Jooles and Chris in tow, our friends from New Mexico. They'd moved into our place a few weeks before after their US visas ran out. All three of them wandered around the track whilst I was doing additional tests, which were more timed laps and an interview with a panel of judges who asked me more questions about racing terminology. I remember one of the finalists – my main competition – was a butch-looking lady with cropped hair. Which one of us would win?

The telephone call came a week later. I'd actually done the impossible and won the racing car! After I put the phone down in stunned silence, I danced around, shrieking with delight. Dave was laughing as he pulled me in for a hug. "You've done it, I knew you would." To celebrate, he took me out for a posh dinner and a bottle of champers at the Manor House Hotel.

The next day, we attended a special presentation at Brands Hatch where I'd won twenty-five lessons from a racing pro which I could have throughout the year. And then I collected my prize – a white Formula Ford racing car with *SHE* emblazoned on the front in red letters to promote the magazine that had launched the competition. Brooke Bond Brazilian Blend who sponsored it was plastered over one side. Holy Moly, I'd not only won a fast car, but I was going to become a fully-fledged racing driver competing against men. It was the biggest high I'd ever experienced. If I hadn't kept a scrapbook of press cuttings from all those years ago, I'd have wondered if I'd dreamt it. How did that happen to little old me?

The publicity meant I had to be media-ready, so I was booked into Vidal Sassoon's to get me spruced up for the press photos. The salon wanted to cut my long hair into the latest trend, the short geometrical style of the time. When I said, "No way, you're not cutting my hair," the stylist shrugged and reluctantly put my locks into big rollers instead to at least make it look bouncy and glamorous.

Heading towards the track, dressed in a red fire-retardant jumpsuit with a white strip down both legs, I was surrounded by reporters and photographers along with the CEO from *She* Magazine

Afterwards, at a nearby hotel, I guzzled back some fizz as we had a champagne lunch in my honour – forty-odd people – journalists and big wigs from the press and the racing world, all mingling around a long table with a finger buffet laden with sausage rolls, little triangle sandwiches, prawn vol-au-vents, and cheese straws.

I held Dave's hand feeling on top of the world. Fame and fortune awaited. Or so I thought …

CHAPTER SIXTEEN

The Drugs Bust

News about my win was plastered all over the local papers – *The Citizen, The Western Daily Press, and The Gloucestershire Echo* along with *The Motorcycle News* because of Dave's fame where I was known as his wife on the circuit. I still worked in the newsagents, so customers would congratulate me when they came in.

But as with everything in my life, drama didn't take long to appear.

Soon after Chris and Jooles moved in, Dave and Chris, started a dope dealing business and parcels began arriving from the U.S. The best hash was hidden in bags inside huge music tapes – four times the size of a standard music cassette. They grew cannabis plants in a locked room with lamps strung up above the marijuana to help them to grow strong as they needed heat and light. I wasn't best pleased that they were dealing after my awful experience with Ray, but Dave was the one paying for everything, so I just kept quiet.

A few weeks after winning the car, Dave was working at the garage, and I was still in bed when I got an early morning call from Chris.

"Have you cleaned the house yet?" he said.

"What are you talking about?" I answered sleepily.

"Mary, listen carefully," he continued. "I'm at the police station. If you haven't cleaned everywhere, do it now!"

The phone went dead.

I quickly twigged that this was a drugs bust and wondered if the police would barge their way in at any moment. Bloody hell, this was serious. We could all be arrested. I quickly got dressed and flew around the house, clearing the roaches out of the fire grate and emptying bins and ashtrays. Then I checked the locked bureau in the dining room – a hash stash of the very best black and Nepalese oil – the amounts split into smaller cellophane bags ready for distribution – a quarter ounce, a half ounce or an ounce.

In a panic, I stuffed all the little bags into my handbag, smoke rising from my heels as I ran out of the house and through the church yard across from where we lived and stashed it all in a friend's barn full of bales of hay.

On the way back, I realised I didn't have the door key! With my heart thudding, I retraced my steps, searching everywhere, losing more and more time. Finally, I found it on top of a hay bale, so I grabbed it and sprinted back home.

Once back in the flat, in blind panic, I unlocked the office door where there were thirty small marijuana plants. More evidence to get rid of! Ripping them up by their roots, I shoved them into a plastic Tesco bag. Then I filled some black bin liners with water bubble pipes, Rizlas, and any other paraphernalia linked to weed.

Loaded down with all the bags, not knowing what else to do with them, I slung them all into the V.W. camper van belonging to Chris and Jooles which was parked in a garage a few doors along. Then I had to get to J.B. Motors to warn Dave who was clearly none the wiser.

Jumping into the driver's seat of the camper van, I turned the ignition with my foot on the accelerator. It stalled. "No, for effs sake, not now," I cried.

Then as I looked through the windscreen, Chris was coming towards the flat in the distance, his arms held on either side by police officers. His eyes swivelled in my direction, and his face said it all, he'd been busted whilst working at his job for Jaguar.

I broke into a sweat. Thank God the police didn't clock me as the garage was separate from the house, so I could have been any one of our neighbours. But the bags of drugs were in the van with me. How much more incriminating could that be? Somehow, I had to move the VW out of the tight space, but I was shaking so hard my foot kept sliding off the clutch, and I ended up smacking the van into the wall of the bakery next door. Thankfully, no damage was done, and amazingly no one came out to see what was going on, but I later discovered the van bumper was hanging off.

Finally, turning the ignition again with shaky hands, the engine revved this time, and I was able to drive towards town feeling as if I'd escaped from Colditz. Pulling up to a red phone box in a layby, I jumped out of the van with the Tesco bag of marijuana plants, and called Dave, planning to dump them afterwards into a nearby rubbish bin.

"Okay, just get here and we'll work it out," he said, his voice quaking.

But as I talked to him on the phone, I could see through the phone box window that a police car was pulling up behind the camper van.

Shit, I'm done for now.

Putting the phone down and shaking like a leaf, I did my best to pick up the bags in a composed manner like a seasoned criminal and walked back towards the vehicle. "Hello," I said to the officer, bright and breezy.

"Hello," replied the copper as I stretched out my arms for him to handcuff me. But he walked right past me and into the phone box.

Phew. With legs like jelly, I managed to get back into the VW with the evidence and sped off to J.B. Autos.

Once I'd parked up, I raced inside clutching the bag of drugs and handed it to Dave. He disposed of it somehow, and then sat me down, his face white as a sheet whilst his father phoned the police station to find out why Chris had been arrested. Meanwhile, one of his mechanics, made me a strong coffee as I was shaking and desperate to keep under the radar. I remained in the garage all day long drinking copious amounts of caffeine.

A few hours later, Dave got a call. In clearing the house of drugs, I hadn't found Chris's 'secret stash' in his bedroom, so he'd been charged for possession. The police had also intercepted another illegal package from the US. Fortunately, Dave's dad, Jack, stood bail for Chris, so he only spent one night in the clink.

Meanwhile, the police forensically searched our house and confiscated all our passports. When Chris walked in, he stormed towards me, looking bedraggled and angry. "Why didn't you find my bloody stash? It's all your fault I've been locked in a cell."

I was on the verge of tears. "I'm sorry, I was on my own, but I did my best to look everywhere."

He glared at me. "Well, you're lucky my phone call saved you all from being arrested!"

Jooles stayed with her mother a lot of the time, but when she returned a few days later and found out what had happened, she just shrugged her shoulders as if it was just one of those things. She was a bit of a strange chick who barely spoke. Maybe she just didn't have much to say or was stoned all the time.

On top of the stress of being arrested, I was worried that this incident would scupper my new racing career. I mean can you imagine the headlines? *Winner of the She Racing Car Competition in Drugs Scandal!*

Sure enough, the story hit the local papers with our address given in full. Thankfully, the drugs were addressed to Chris, so we weren't incriminated or brought into the station, and the article only cited Chris's full name, showing that he was arrested whilst residing at our address, so we were off the hook.

Our landlord then got in touch to insist our friends vacated the premises and I was beyond grateful. Trouble seemed to follow us around, so, it was with relief that we'd somehow wriggled out of yet another conundrum.

What I didn't know then is that things would get far worse than either of us could have ever predicted.

CHAPTER SEVENTEEN

November 10th, 1974

The Accident that Changed our Lives Forever

It was a cold, miserable night when we attended Dave's cousin's 21st birthday party at her house in Cheltenham. I didn't fancy going. Apart from the fact it was freezing, all Dave's old racing cronies were coming, and I didn't know any of them. But I put on some glad rags and make-up and did what I felt was expected of me.

When we got there, the place was packed, as we squeezed past crowds of noisy people to head to the kitchen, music pounding with the sounds of Led Zeplin. I poured myself a glass of cider and Dave got a whiskey from the counter when suddenly five men appeared all shoving their way towards my boyfriend, pointing and shouting, "It's old Davey boy, the great superstar."

"Are they part of your racing crowd?" I asked Dave as I sipped my drink.

"Yep," he said with a smirk, "my competitors on the tracks."

The men all stood around us making general chit-chat, but as the drink flowed, they all seemed to get louder and louder, their teasing turning into taunts.

"Is this your bird, Davey boy," said a tall guy, glancing at me and then squaring his shoulders in an intimating way. "Did you tell her your championship was fixed?"

"Yeah, I was much better than you," said another shorter bloke whilst the others all laughed.

I wasn't worried at that point as I knew Dave could take a joke, and initially, he replied with a smirk, "Yeah, right, guys. You're all just jealous." But with all the beer, whiskey and weed, the comments between them became more vitriolic.

"You paid the sponsors off, didn't you? We all know, you could barely drive a bumper car," continued the tall guy with a sneer.

"Shut the fuck up," snapped Dave, swigging back another whiskey.

I looked at him feeling nervous with all this ego-fuelled testosterone flying around, and that's when I saw a side of Dave I hadn't seen before – his face a beetroot red, and his fists clenched as he leaned forward staring right into one of the guys faces. Then, one of his rivals shoved him and he shoved them back.

It was around 1.30 a.m., and I was scared things were getting out of hand, so I tapped Dave on the arm and said, "Can we go?"

He staggered slightly and gave me a blank look. I don't think he realised I was still there, he was so inebriated, but hearing my voice seemed to sober him up a little and he nodded.

Outside in the darkness, it was tipping down with rain as we both clambered into his red jag, although he seemed to have trouble getting in and then dropped the keys on the wet ground. After scrambling around to pick them up, he sat in front of the steering wheel with hate in his eyes and I was really frightened. I knew he was stoned and way over the limit. Driving was the last thing he should be doing.

"Shall we get a cab back instead? You can pick your car up tomorrow," I said, my voice shaky.

"No!" he said, "I'm fine."

Well, that put me in my place, so I decided it was best to keep schtum. But I was worried about how he'd navigate his way through all the cars parked everywhere in their driveway, and my concerns were right. When he started the ignition and tried to steer his way out, the jag lurched forward, and he hit a few of the motors in front of him. It was obvious he'd caused some damage, dented someone's bumper and the door of another car, but he was so drunk, I don't think he was even aware of it. And without a backward glance, he sped off.

Thankfully the roads were quiet in the early hours, but he was skidding all over the place and I thought he was going to crash, so in a state of panic, half a mile down the road when we came to a T junction, I screamed, "I want to get out. Let me out."

Dave abruptly stopped the car, flung open my door, and said, "Get out then!"

I looked at the dark road ahead of me and had second thoughts. I didn't want to be left abandoned in the rain in the middle of the night, so I closed the door and bolstered myself for whatever fate had in store.

"I'm fine," he reiterated, "I *will* get us home."

But my stomach churned.

I held my breath, relieved that there wasn't a single car around on our ten-mile journey home until Dave veered onto the wrong side of the road. With my heart in my throat, I put my feet on the dashboard to steady myself. Then Dave went around a hairpin bend where there was a blind spot and before I could think straight, he'd smashed into another car coming the opposite way.

I must have passed out, because the next thing I remember was coming round in the passenger seat to the sound of sirens with blood trickling down my face, my whole body numb. Someone had covered me with their coat, which meant this was real, not some horrible nightmare that I could wake up from. But where was Dave? I slowly managed to turn my head and saw that the crash had flipped him somehow – he was unconscious, lying sprawled across the top of the driver's seat as if he was on a slope, his head at a strange angle.

Unable to move much, I felt a surge of panic as I screamed, "Wake up, Dave. Please wake up."

It all felt like it had happened in slow motion – the bend, the swerve, the rain, the darkness, the collision. I was crying in pain, and someone gave me oxygen and a jab of something. And I don't remember anything else until the paramedics put me on a stretcher.

"Is Dave, okay? He's not dying, is he?" I asked them repeatedly. And they reassured me that he was still breathing but that it didn't look good at this stage.

Oh, God! Why did we go out? Why did he drive? I couldn't stop crying, knowing that Dave might die.

The following morning, I woke up in a hospital bed with blood-caked hair and bruised ribs and discovered I had a bad head injury needing eight stitches. I felt sorry for myself, but I was more concerned about Dave. And by some weird coincidence, I realised the accident happened right by Cranham woods where his mother had killed herself.

I asked again where Dave was and a nurse told me that he was being moved to I.C.U. in Frenchay Hospital, Bristol where they had more neurological expertise and equipment.

Shit. He had to be in a bad way. I was desperate to see him, but I wasn't allowed as he was in such a critical condition. All I could do is watch anxiously through the window in front of me as his unconscious body was wheeled into the ambulance on a stretcher.

I was also told by one of the nurses that the driver of the car Dave collided with, as well as the three passengers, all suffered broken limbs, which I knew he'd be devasted about if he knew. And the police didn't pursue anything after hearing that Dave might only have twenty-four hours to live.

I felt terribly guilty for the other casualties as well as what had happened to Dave, despite not being the one behind the wheel. All the awful things that happened that evening came rushing back – the arguments, the taunting, the loud music, and excessive drinking. If only I hadn't said this or done that. I expect we can all look back on our lives and think 'If only!'

Discharging myself two days later, I was determined to visit Dave. I couldn't bear the thought of going back to our home without him, but because of my injuries, I wasn't able to work for a while, and therefore couldn't pay the rent on our place in Painswick. And not being his wife, I had no access to his finances. This also meant that without access to our old garage next door, I had to frantically ring around friends, and finally got my Formula Ford racing car stored in a barn on a friend's farm.

In a panic, I phoned Dave's father, Jack, and he invited me to move in with him and Carol. It was a challenging time as Jack had suffered a stroke a couple of weeks before Dave's accident and was still slowly recovering. All of this put an awful strain on Carol as well as Dave's sister, Lynne who was now four months pregnant. The only thing to do was carry on as best we could.

The next day, Jack and Carol took me to see Dave in Bristol and I froze when I saw him. He was in a coma in ICU with monitors attached to his body and he'd had a tracheotomy – a hole in his throat with a tube inserted into this windpipe to help him breathe and eat.

The doctors told us that he'd suffered severe brain damage but to what extent they didn't know. Jack stared at his son dumbstruck while I sobbed my heart out. He looked so bruised and fragile. This was my soul mate, the perfect gentleman who made me feel loved for the very first time, and now, I didn't know if I'd lost him forever in some limbo state or if he'd die.

I couldn't bear to be away from him, so I drove myself up there every day in my little MG and sat by his bed. "Dave, please wake up!" I'd say repeatedly.

CHAPTER EIGHTEEN

Keeping the Faith

Eight weeks passed, the Christmas and New Year celebrations making me feel even more miserable as I continued to sit beside him daily, desperate for a sign. Thankfully, he was transferred to a private room, but I was shocked by his rapid decline. He'd always had a muscular physique, but although he was still being fed by a tube, he'd lost around four stone in weight, his bones protruding through his skin. And scarily, his body was contracting, including his arms and legs as he curled into a foetal position. The doctors confirmed that spasticity had set in all over which apparently can happen with brain damage.

Seeing him so regularly, many things gave me cause for concern. The nurses had fitted him with a catheter, but he got an infection, so they put a plastic bottle in the bed beside him with his penis inside it, for the urine. On numerous occasions, the bed would be soaking wet whenever he'd moved slightly, and the bottle had slipped off. He was also getting infection after infection on his chest and had terrible choking fits where he went blue in the face. Despite being in a coma, he'd thrash his legs and arms around and even tugged his trachea tube out. That was clearly a sign that the tube was uncomfortable, but the doctors stated he couldn't survive without it, so they tied his hands to the side of the bed so that it wouldn't happen again.

There were moments when Dave opened his eyes and stared into the distance, but when I told the doctors excitedly, they said that it wasn't significant. They'd also done an MRI and found a blood clot in the mid part of his brain. "His chances of survival aren't good," said the doctor, talking to me afterwards. "And if he does survive, there's a good chance he'll be a vegetable."

I was beyond devastated. It felt as if they'd all given up on him. But I certainly wouldn't give up, whatever the outcome. I wanted to be there for him as he'd always been there for me. So, I kept talking to him, reading the motorcycle news to him or telling him about his sister's new baby hoping part of him would hear me and wake up.

This is one of the first letters I wrote to my brother Pat and his wife Jean.

2nd January 1975

Dear Pat and Jean,

Just a short note to let you know that I'm OK. I've just got over the horrid bug although it's left me a little down in the dumps. Still, I suppose that will soon pass.

Dave is still the same, although he isn't responding as well as he was. He was having fits about a week ago but has calmed down now. I seem to be coping with everything as life goes on, although it's the hardest thing I've ever faced. I still can't believe it's happened to us. It's like being in a nightmare and expecting to wake up and have everything back to normal.

Carolyn, my mate who has the cottage in Leckhampton Hill, is coming home in a few weeks from Leeds where she's been working. So, I shall probably go and live with her which will be a lot better. Jack and Carol are really looking after me, but it's a bit like living at home with the folks – the News is always on TV, and I find myself creeping up the stairs at 10.30 p.m. after being out for the evening, trying not to wake them. They're usually in bed around nine. Still, they've been very kind to me, and I have a lot to thank them for. But there's nowhere quite like your own home is there?

I feel so lost all the time, but I guess that's because part of me remains in Bristol. But I'm certain that one day, Dave will wake up.

I'm taking his two children to the pictures tomorrow. They're both dealing with it quite well, although, they keep asking when they can see Daddy, but I don't think it's wise to take them as it might frighten them. Dave just doesn't look like himself at the moment. He has a tube up his nose and a tracheostomy. Do you think it would upset them or do you think it's more important for them to see that their father is, putting it bluntly, still alive? I haven't a clue, but Jean, you know a lot about children. I need your advice on that one.

Anyway, I won't write anymore as I tend to get a bit tired. I've enclosed some of your wedding photos. They are lovely. Have you got any that I could have? Just a couple with perhaps one with Dave and me. Don't worry about getting any done specially, it was just a thought.
Much love to you both,
Mary xxx
PS. I hope you had a good Christmas and wish you a Happy New Year.

1975 – Back to Reality

The long forty-mile drive every day was taking its toll. I was exhausted. Family and friends gave me help and encouragement, but I just wanted Dave back home with me safe and sound.

In March, three months later, there appeared to be a breakthrough.

I kissed him goodbye, and this time, he tilted his face up and kissed me back – a long slow kiss. I thought I was dreaming but Lynne, who came with me, was in tears having witnessed this miracle. Then, I couldn't stop kissing him. "I know you're OK now my darling!" I spluttered.

With jubilant hearts, we ran to the Sister's Office and told her our good news. I should have known better than to expect her to be as over the moon as I was. What does a kiss mean to anyone if they're not on the receiving end?

She squeezed my shoulder and said, "I expect it was just a coincidence, my love!"

"Come and see for yourself," I replied, as she brought a nurse with her, praying on the way back to Dave's room that it would happen again.

I took a breath, leaned over and kissed him. And bless him, he kissed me back again in front of them. The nurses' eyes widened, finally realising that he really was responding to me.

The doctors were informed and the next morning, they performed another brain scan which revealed that the blood clot had dispersed, which meant that Dave stood an even better chance of survival – but they confirmed that despite his reaction, he was still in a coma.

I was upset that they didn't believe me, no doubt thinking it was all in my imagination. But I knew deep down that the kiss meant Dave was aware somehow of my presence. And that gave me hope.

In between visits, I had many other things to deal with: bills to pay and more letters to write to let my brother and mum know what was going on, so I'd sit up in bed half the night scribbling away until I fell asleep. I'd wake up still clutching a pen or a notepad.

A week on, there was still no further progress, Dave's vital signs going up and down like a yo-yo. The doctors decided it would be best if he was transferred back to Gloucester Hospital as there wasn't much more they could do for him.

My throat tightened. Why were they sending him back? Was it to die? During my three months of visits, I'd seen many patients have their life support switched off and I prayed that wouldn't happen to my Dave.

My friend Margaret came to visit him with me before the move. I knew her and her partner Chris from my wild hippy days, and she just happened to be a staff nurse at Cheltenham hospital. She told me to look at things positively, and that at least Gloucester would be far more convenient.

In truth, she was right; it would only be ten miles away from Cheltenham, instead of the forty-odd miles to Bristol.

Two weeks later at Gloucester, the doctors began to slowly wean Dave off all the meds he was on, and he seemed to stir a little more and open his mouth for food. Despite him still not being aware of his surroundings, I wanted to arrange a little birthday celebration for his thirtieth on March 17th.

Stringing up all his cards, I hung them around his headboard, along with some balloons. Margaret made an iced fruit cake and all of us including Dave's sister, Lynne, along with a few of the nurses, sang happy birthday to him, as I yelled, "Welcome to the flirty thirties."

Then low and behold, he suddenly opened his eyes, lifted his head off the pillow and grunted out, "Excuse me, I'm only twenty-nine!" At least that's what I could tell he wanted to holler – but what came out was this breathless, almost childlike: *"Excuuuth meeee, I'm onyy twenthhhyyyniinnnne!"*

We were all dumbstruck, and everyone had tears in their eyes, overcome with emotion after wondering if he'd ever wake up.

I went over and hugged him, and in his eyes, I could see that he recognised me, even if he couldn't smile yet because of his damaged facial muscles, but that twinkle in his eyes said everything.

His outburst had an astonishing effect on the hospital staff. The consultant was called by the nurse and within twenty-four hours a team moved in – speech therapists, physiotherapists, clinical psychologists, and social workers, who ensured from then on that he was given every assistance available.

I was beyond elated. Dave was finally awake after four months. We could gradually start to rebuild our lives.

CHAPTER NINETEEN

I Can See Clearly Now the Rain Has Gone

In between visits, I wrote to my friend Carolyn to explain everything that happened. Over the last two years, she'd separated from her husband, Derek, leaving him in the cottage, 'Here-we-are', and got a live-in pub job in Yorkshire. But when she got my letter, unbeknownst to me, she promptly walked out on her job and returned home. Then, she asked her ex-husband to move out and invited me to move in.

I was so astonished at the huge sacrifice she made. I mean, seriously, if Heineken made friends … I was so relieved as I was under a strict regime with Jack and Carol where I cooked and cleaned as my contribution for staying there but I also had to be in by a certain time. It was like being back with my parents, not having my own life.

Moving back in with Carolyn would bring some support as well as some much-needed laughter back into my life.

Here's another letter to my brother, giving him an update.

15th February 1975

Dear Jean and Pat,

Thanks ever so much for your letter. I'm sorry I've taken so long to write but as you can imagine, I just never seem to have the time to put pen to paper.

Dave is at present in Gloucester Hospital which is much better as I can spend more time with him. Evidentially it was the best thing that happened as the Bristol lot didn't seem to bother with him. The doctors at Glos. were very distressed as he'd lost three stones in weight. They told me that Bristol had just given him up as no good.

As soon as they got him to Glos. they gave him a hot bath which seemed to stir him and ever since then he's improved, very slowly, but there's a big difference in him – he's awake for most of the day and he recognises me.

Last week, he uttered a few words, so the Speech Therapist visits him twice a week and he's able to say quite a few things now. They think his vocal cords are a little paralysed so he's having trouble getting sound out. But he's certainly a lot better than when I last spoke to you. His arms were what they called at the time, spastic, in that they turned in on themselves, a bit like someone with cerebral palsy. He can, at least, move his left hand which is a start. I think, in time, lots of physiotherapy will get them working. In all honesty, it's going to be a long while before Dave is better but it doesn't matter how long because I'm sure one day he will be.

I'm living with Carolyn's parents at the moment, and next week, we're moving into the cottage on Leckhampton Hill. I'm much happier now and coping with things well. Carolyn has become a great help to me.

We both started work at Wall's Ice Cream Factory two weeks ago on a night shift, but we only lasted a week and a half as it seemed like slave labour. So, I'm looking for another part-time job.

Thanks, Jean, for the advice about the children. It's Dave's birthday next month, so I think it would be a good idea to take his sons to see him. He's definitely looking more like their old dad again.

I'm glad you've got another car as judging from the phone conversations with Pat, it sounded as though your old one was on its last legs. Mine's also on its way out. Everything seems to be going wrong with it. Still, I suppose they can't last forever.

I'm also going to have to sell the racing car I won from She Magazine as it doesn't look as though I'll ever be able to race it. Besides, the money will come in useful for when Dave comes out of hospital.

Our story about it all will be in the April edition of She Magazine. They postponed putting it in earlier because of our accident as they thought it would upset me too much. That was really very nice of them. They also sent me a huge bouquet and sent Dave numerous 'Get Well' cards. Everybody has been so kind ... even people I don't know.

Anyway, I'll close now as I could ramble on forever. When I move up to the cottage, I'll ring you from there. But I won't be there for another week.

I hope you're both well and not working too hard.

Love to you both,

Mary xxx

CHAPTER TWENTY

The Three Musketeers

Six months after the accident, Dave was progressing well, but he still couldn't talk properly because the tracheostomy had damaged his vocal cords, so he'd grunt his way through a sentence, which while confusing to a stranger, I got used to understanding. And amazingly, I knew he understood me too, as, in response, his eyes would light up.

Things were definitely on the upturn with regards to his health and Dave was well on the road to coming home. Carolyn and I looked forward to getting him rehabilitated outside the hospital. I, for one, couldn't wait. I just loved him so much and wanted to take control of his care. The problem was age-old sexism. In those days, medical staff wouldn't address me if they were changing Dave's medication or had updates on his care; they'd only address his father, Jack, simply because I wasn't his wife. And yet, I was the one who'd lived with him for four years and knew him better than anyone else.

So, I made a huge decision that I'd been mulling over for weeks. Sitting by Dave's bedside, I leaned over to touch his hand and gazed into his eyes, my heart racing. "Darling Dave, I love you so much. Will you marry me?"

I'll always remember how surprised he looked as his eyes widened and then filled with tears. I don't think he could actually believe that I'd want to be with him given the circumstances. But I did, desperately. When you love someone, truly love them, you'll do anything to facilitate their happiness. And I wanted to do exactly that, pick up the broken bones of him and make him well. And in response, he gave me a lopsided grin, and choked out the words: "Yes, please."

Why on God's earth did I propose to him, you might well ask? A young woman of twenty-four lumbering myself with an invalid who could never give her a 'normal' marriage. And many would agree with you, including Carolyn's mother.

The morning of our wedding, six weeks later, I lay in the bath full of bubbles with a stiff brandy as she sat on the loo seat beside me. "You know it's not too late to pull out, Mary," she said, locking eyes with me.

I rubbed my face with wet, soapy hands. "Are you kidding? No way. I want to marry him. He's my soul mate."

She gave me a soft smile and leaned forward. "Well then, you're either a fool or a saint."

But I was neither. I was simply a girl in love.

Dave's first trip out into the big world outside the sterile world of hospitals was the day we got married in Gloucester registry office. It was the most beautiful spring morning in May, so we picked sprigs of cherry blossom and attached them with ribbon to Carolyn's car. Earlier, Chris, Margaret's partner, had gone over to the hospital to get Dave dressed in a suit and plonked in a wheelchair. It was a small affair – around twenty people, but close friends and family were all that mattered.

After we'd exchanged vows, there was a reception at Dave's grandfather's three-storey Victorian house, simply because he and his second wife had the space – although the grimace on Dad's face said it all. No doubt, he was still annoyed that I wasn't incarcerated in a convent, and now I'd married a disabled man. My brother, Pat, and Mum were naturally happy for me, but then they'd always supported me through everything and knew I was doing my best.

I was thrilled that Pat came. As you saw earlier, we mainly corresponded through letters, but a few years before, I'd attended his registry office nuptials to his soul mate Jean. Their wedding was held in the lake district with only six of us – Dave and I, Pat's best mate from uni, and a girlfriend of Jean's.

It was the first time I'd seen Jean and my mouth dropped open. She wore a floor-length white dress with a matching floppy hat, and she looked like my doppelganger – long dark hair, around five foot five, and a size eight figure. I could see from her little nod and smile that she spotted the similarity too. Now I was reunited with my brother again, only this time, he came alone as Jean didn't know anyone else there.

After the celebrations were over, I didn't want to take Dave straight back to the hospital, so we planned a 'honeymoon' overnight stay with Chris and Margaret. Gloucester hospital wouldn't usually allow a patient out overnight but because Margaret was a staff nurse at Cheltenham General and therefore had some clout, I was able to sign a form stating that I'd take full responsibility if anything happened to him.

From then on, Dave moved forward with monumental strides. After lots of physio and speech therapy, he could vocalise a little better, although an outsider would struggle to understand.

Carolyn was my partner in crime, and together, we'd pick him up from the hospital in his wheelchair and then venture off on our mad adventures. First, we'd head back to Carolyn's on a Friday evening in a blue and white Hillman Avenger, bouncing up the rough track up to her cottage, surrounded by the breathtaking views of the town and the surrounding Malvern and Cleeve Hills.

Carolyn's crazy cocker spaniel, Tumbleweed, would greet us, barking and jumping up just as we tried to heave a six-foot-two man out of the passenger seat. This was no mean feat. There was Carolyn, five foot nothing, and me, only a few inches taller, each holding his arm on either side to get him up to a standing position. Then we'd stagger through the wrought iron gate with him as we couldn't get the wheelchair through.

Once inside, we'd plonk a wobbly Dave into an armchair with a beer next to him. Carolyn would have dinner ready, and the weekend would begin, full of obstacles, hilarity, and adventures.

Donning straw hats and a picnic basket, we visited Burford Wildlife Park. I pushed Dave in his wheelchair whilst Carolyn was loaded up with everything she could carry – Tupperware boxes filled with boiled eggs, ham, cheese, and French sticks as well as China plates, cutlery, mugs, and a large flask of tea.

We found a perfect spot in a rose garden surrounded by three privet hedges. I shoved a tartan blanket down on the grass and put a small collapsible table on Dave's lap. Unfortunately, Dave often had choking fits. The tracheostomy had left him with dysphagia, so I'd be smacking him on his back as a piece of bread flew out like a red arrow.

Another time, we drove to a pub called 'The Air Balloon,' just under a mile away. It was called that because the place was set on Birdlip hill where you could look down onto the valley. Dave was growing more independent and decided he wanted to walk from the car park to the beer garden which should, in reality, only take a few minutes. Taking hold of him on either side, Carolyn and I lurched, staggered, and stumbled as Dave in his eager pursuit to make it to an available outside table was off like a greyhound.

The pub was heaving with crowds of people, children, and dogs. When Dave was finally seated at a table and safe, we pushed our way through to the bar to order two pints of beer and a pint of lager.

The landlady who was blonde and busty with bright red lipstick came over to speak to us with a serious expression on her face. "You two ladies can both have a drink," she said, "but not that drunk man with you!" Apparently, she'd seen him staggering about through the window.

"He's not drunk," I said firmly, "he's brain damaged from an accident and only just come out of a coma."

The landlady frowned but relented, no doubt, feeling a little embarrassed that she'd made such a huge assumption.

As for Dave, well he overheard and smirked. I knew for once that he was happy to be seen as a drunk and not a cripple.

A month later, Dave was transferred to Standish Hospital near Glos. fifteen miles away for intensive physiotherapy, speech and learning skills for his contorted arms.

Although we were both welcome at Carolyn's cottage, there wasn't enough space, so we had no home for us to live in as a married couple.

Social services, fortunately, got involved and found us a two-bed ground floor council flat in Prestbury near Cheltenham racecourse. It was wheelchair friendly and had grab rails at the front door and in the bathroom. I eventually bought it for around two thousand pounds a few years later. Unbelievable when you think of property prices now.

Carolyn had a new boyfriend, Colin, who she eventually married, and they both helped decorate our new place in magnolia to make it look fresh and clean.

Naturally, my racing dreams were in the gutter, but I sold my racing car for two thousand, five hundred pounds – an enormous amount of money in the seventies. And that provided us with furniture, carpets, a double bed, a sofa, and crockery etc. To make it even more of a home for Dave, his old trophies soon arrived from storage.

Dave was discharged on September 10th, 1975 – ten months to the very day since the accident. And with huge excitement, after our place was finally ready, we moved into our new home.

But there was no rest for the wicked. Dave was kept busy with speech therapy and physio, and I was desperately trying to find a job. It was a challenge for him to get around. He was using a wheelchair which we had to push as he still had one arm bending towards his body, so he couldn't rotate the wheels himself, and he still struggled to vocalise any speech.

One morning, I heard banging on the door. Wondering who it was, I tentatively opened it. Dave was having treatment, so I was alone, and at first, I didn't register who this strange woman was on my doorstep – overweight and scruffy with unkempt mousy hair.

Without introducing herself, she blurted out, "I need money, I've got rent to pay, school uniforms and food. I can't support the children on my own any longer."

I realised this was Dave's ex and the mother of his kids. I was surprised that she'd been his type. She was a formidable character and there was an overriding sense of aggression as if she might lash out at me.

I winced. How could I help out when we were living on the bare minimum, juggling work with taking care of Dave? "Umm, I don't have any money," I said nervously. "Dave's still in and out of hospital. We're just about surviving ourselves."

"Get him to ask his dad then," she said, glaring at me.

I shook my head. "I'm sorry but we've got our own challenges. You'll have to ask his father yourself."

She didn't look happy, her face pinched as she looked me up and down, and then stomped off. I was relieved that she'd gone without slapping me around the face.

Not long after, tragedy struck again. Late one evening, around ten, there was a knock on the door from the police. Dave was already in bed asleep. Delivering more bad news, they told me that Dave's father, Jack, had died of a heart attack at Heathrow Airport whilst returning from Alicante with his wife and family. He was only fifty-three!

I was shell-shocked. *What's next?* Jack was a funny, supportive man regardless of his misdemeanours, but it seemed to be one tragedy after another, and I was worried sick about telling Dave. But I knew it was better done sooner than later.

After the police had gone, I went into our bedroom and sat on the side of the bed. Dave opened his eyes and gazed at me.

"Sweetheart, I've got some bad news, I'm afraid." I inhaled, my stomach clenching. "Your dad's had a heart attack and died."

Dave stared at me, and then he choked up, spluttering, trying to make sounds, but still unable to vocalise how he felt. I leaned over and hugged him as he lay his head against my shoulder. The poor guy had already been through the wringer, and now most of his family had been annihilated. How would I get him through this?

Telling his sister, Lynne, was an even bigger challenge, knowing her mental instability. I had to be tactful.

Dave and I met her husband, Merv, at the garage where he was a motor mechanic and we all drove to their house together. Merv got Lynne to sit down again as he always did, trying to prepare her. "I'm so sorry, my love, but your father's dead."

Lynne went very quiet and stared at all three of us again with disbelief. We both waited, knowing that she took a lot of meds and always seemed to be in a bit of a fog, not knowing if the news had sunk in.

"Lynne, I'm so sorry, but this is the reality, and we can't change it," I said as I knelt by her side and held her hand. Her husband tried to put his arm around her, but she pushed him away. I went into the kitchen to put the kettle on, but the hot, sweet tea brought zero comfort, and before I left, it broke my heart to hear her sobbing hysterically.

A week later, we attended his father's funeral, three years after his mother's death.

CHAPTER TWENTY-ONE

Turning Things Around

On a positive note, amidst all this sadness, I finally got a new job working with Dave's stepmother, Carol, in her shop called 'Things' on Cheltenham high street. J.B. Motors and Son was around twenty shops away which she and Jack had turned into a second-hand furniture shop. Now she was running the place alone, collecting and selling larger items such as wardrobes, beds, and settees from house clearances. I became a junk expert, learning the business on the job as I'd get the smaller items like pictures, lamps, crockery, jewellery, and books, cleaning and fixing them if necessary.

The pub across the road became my lunchtime watering hole where I became friends with the pub landlady, Jane, and her husband. She was in her fifties and like a mum to me, often bringing me a coffee and a sandwich if I was busy. Boy, did I need friends back then, just to get me through the day.

Once more I wrote to my brother to update him on everything and was relieved to have some family unity and make peace with my father.

21ˢᵗ November 1975

Dear Pat and Jean,

Mum and Dad came to stay with us on Dad's birthday. I didn't know whether Dad would accept our invite, but surprisingly he did. He must have had a change of heart, maybe because Mum had a word with him or maybe he just realised that I was in a challenging situation and trying to make the best of things. It made me feel more of a sense of family solidarity for once. And, by golly, we had quite a booze up at the local pub. Mum and I had a fair bit of wine, and Dad had his whiskey which cheered him up. Then Dad passed out on the settee and Mum slept on a blow-up bed on the floor! I don't think they were very comfortable, but it made a change for them, and I think it did them both good. The only thing missing was you two.

I can't think of anything to buy them for Christmas. Mum's not so hard to buy for, but Dad, well, it's almost impossible. They seem to be all right for everything. If I do have any bright ideas, I'll let you know.

Dave is well. He says hello and sends his love. He'll be going to Rivermead Rehabilitation Centre soon, before Christmas. It's for eight weeks where they give physio and speech therapy. It all sounds very encouraging anyway. The specialist has also said that he'll do another operation to lower Dave's arm as it's stuck at a ninety-degree angle. Dave's getting very fed up and depressed about the whole thing. He gets frustrated because he can't physically do things. He says, his brain tells him to do it, but the mechanisms just won't work. Still, perhaps, this rehab will do him the world of good. I do hope so.

Other than that, we are very happy. Nothing else to complain about. In fact, life is very good when we think about it. There are always others worse off than yourself.

I do hope you get your PhD, Pat. You've earned it. I think, Jean, you probably deserve one too. Has he been awful to live with? When he was taking his O and A levels, he was a pain in the bum. Still, not a bad brother really. In fact, I think you're both lovely.

Anyway, I will ring you one night when we go to Carolyn's. Dave says you can buy him an E type for Christmas – nothing flashy. He's still determined to have one. You'd think the accident would have put him off. Still, it's good to know that he's still got the bottle to drive.

Look after yourselves,

Much love,

Mary and Dave xxx

Further on into Dave's rehab at Rivermead, the doctor decided Dave needed to challenge himself by being more independent, and that what he really needed to rebuild his health was to achieve something. Anything! On his own! This meant Dave had to find his own way to and from Stanmore on the outskirts of London.

On the one hand, that was great news, as it meant I wouldn't have the arduous two-and-a-half-hour drive. But Dave's journey entailed a bus, two tubes and then a train from Paddington to Cheltenham Spa, so when I knew he'd caught the train for the very first time, my heart was in my mouth, as I waited on the station platform for him to appear. I was relieved when I saw him stumble out of the train door in his big coat with a duffle bag slung across his shoulders.

The consultant from Rivermead also referred Dave for reconstruction on his contorted arm, and shortly afterwards, surgeons took a piece of bone from his hip and grafted it onto his left wrist to straighten it. His right arm was still too contracted, but the operation on the left arm meant he would be able to do much more for himself such as lifting a kettle to make himself a brew or typing on a keyboard.

This newfound independence marked a major turning point in his life. He had a sparkle in his eyes and a huge smile at achieving something major. He was proud of himself, as was I, proving to everyone, that a useful life doesn't have to end after a head injury; it's just different.

He also made some good friends at Rivermead which was so important for his well-being – two guys also undergoing rehab called Eddie and John. We'd stay with them both separately in London for the occasional weekend and vice versa. Eddie lived at home with his mum and brother in Hackney, East London, and had lost his arm in a motorbike accident. And then there was John who lived in a mews house in Barnett. He'd previously worked as a sound technician for Queen and contracted Guillain-Barre Syndrome after getting food poisoning. It had left the poor guy paralysed initially but after rehab, he got back his full mobility.

The two guys told me when they came to visit, that it would be good for Dave's independence to get back behind the wheel of a car! They'd clearly all been talking and persuaded me that in an automatic car, with practice along with his previous experience, all would be well.

Agreeing to this anxiously, I'd drive Dave to a disused airstrip where he could practice safely. With his nerves of steel and dogged determination, he did indeed drive again, six months later in our automatic car.

Around the same time, Headway Gloucester became a big part of our lives. It was an organisation within Gloucester hospital for people with acquired head injuries. It was still in its infancy back then, so they weren't widely known. A married couple approached me after I came to visit Dave one afternoon and asked if we wanted to visit other people with head injuries along with their families to offer any advice that had been useful for us.

I loved the idea of helping others and started volunteer work for them a few weeks later which proved to be immensely rewarding and therapeutic. It opened my eyes to other people's emotional trauma that I could fully empathise with.

I met a woman called Rose in one of the hospital visitor's rooms. She had two children and was struggling as her husband was in a coma. She told me that their marriage was an unhappy one even before her husband's accident. I told her candidly that if life was difficult then, it would only get worse because she'd be his primary carer. I could tell from her unhappy expression that she didn't want to hear the truth. By the same token, she didn't dare leave her husband, feeling guilty that she should keep the family together. It was challenging trying to support her as she was caught between a rock and a hard place.

I also saw a fifteen-year-old lad called Nick with his parents. He was all bent up in a wheelchair and so brain damaged that he'd regressed to a childlike state where he could barely speak. Like so many teenagers, he was fearless and had been playing 'Chicken' running across the road in front of cars, seeing who could go the fastest. Unfortunately, he got knocked over and had a severe head injury. I was there to support his parents and try and give them some hope. It was devastating as I knew from the doctors that the damage was irreversible, and they'd have to be his full-time carers. Two or three years later, sadly he died. But I hoped during our meetings, I gave his parents some way to offload their pain and anguish.

1978 – An Independent Woman

Three years later, when I was twenty-eight, Carol was so busy with her own business, that she gifted the lease of 'Things' to me and Dave. I was thrilled and gave it a fresh rebrand, calling it 'Reflections.' I loved every part of it – going to auctions and people's houses, buying, cleaning, mending, and repairing desirable junk. And making a profit.

The place became my oasis and I felt empowered. I was an independent woman in my own right, rather than just the wife of a disabled man. And it helped get Dave back on his feet again. He'd sit behind the counter, but he was able-bodied enough by now to stand up and stagger towards any customers to help them find something.

I headed to Stratford on Avon and Bristol auctions to expand our stock as well as local auctions in Cheltenham as I mixed with antique dealers, buying and selling amidst crowds of ambitious men. Earls Court Antique Fair was one of the highlights. It was a huge event, where people come from all over the world, where it cost thousands to have a stand, so I got glammed up for it, curling my hair, and wearing a smart trouser suit, my nails painted a glossy red. I'd attend with Carol and her new man who was an antique dealer to sell thousands of pounds worth of antique furniture as I'd chat away with prospective buyers. It gave me a new sense of well-being, so my life wasn't spent revolving around Dave's health.

More Spanish Chaos

With our respective businesses thriving, Carol thought all three of us needed a break, so, she booked a two-bed apartment in Alicante for a week, organising for her two children to stay with their dad.

The swimming pool was in the centre of a huge complex surrounded by blocks of apartments. We were all sitting on a low stone wall by the swimming pool, Carol and I chatting away in our bikinis. Dave was in his swimming trunks next to me, smiling at every pretty girl. He never did lose his love of women or his confidence despite his disability.

As Lou Reed once sang, 'It was such a perfect day' – scorching sun, elated moods, the thundering sound of a waterfall behind us, cooling us down from hot Spanish sun, cold droplets splashing onto our scorched bodies. I had my back to Dave, talking intently to Carol when I heard someone yelling. I turned around to check on Dave and he'd disappeared. Carol and I looked at each other in panic. "Where the hell's Dave gone?" I said, my heart pounding.

We heard a garbled voice yelling again, and as I looked over the other side of the wall, I could see a hand pointing upwards through the water as the waterfall cascaded over his head. It was Dave!

"Oh Christ, let's get you out of there," I cried as Carol rushed forward.

The poor guy had fallen backwards into a three-foot wide gap between the waterfall and the wall and then plummeted to the bottom where the water was being pumped back to the top. Despite him being so much more able-bodied, it was clear we couldn't take our eyes off him for a second.

I looked at Carol and we both leaned over trying to grab an arm each to haul him out, but he was far too heavy. Luckily the gap was only seven feet deep, but the water was getting lower as it was being recycled into the pool, so it was big enough for his six-foot-two frame to get wedged in, but not to actually drown. I didn't know what to do for the best as he continued to gasp for air as the waterfall continued to pour over his head.

"HELP! HELP!" he continued to yell, vocalising as much as he could with his limited vocabulary. It was a busy place with tourists turning to stare at us whilst they were sunbathing or swimming. Then a maintenance guy must have seen what happened and came over to help haul him out.

After he got him safely on dry land, Dave's eyes were wide open, his face dripping wet as he started to laugh. It was a common reaction, the hysteria and shock of having yet another accident. He had grazes to his elbows and knees and a gash on his head, but they looked superficial, so we didn't feel we needed to cart him off to hospital. He was obviously wobbly, though, so we got him seated at a nearby table and quickly cleaned up any blood with our towels and then sprayed him with insect repellent! The last thing we needed was him getting bitten on top of all his cuts and bruises. Once we'd got him sorted, exhausted with trying to keep him out of danger, we all made our way to the bar for a much-needed drink amidst quizzical looks of concern.

This kind of chaos with an accident-prone Dave seemed to ensue anytime we went anywhere. Some old friends of mine, a couple called Lucy and George, invited Dave and me to stay for a two-week holiday with them in the Algarve. They'd lived there for two years looking after the most beautiful three-storey villa for an elderly gentleman who used it as his occasional getaway. It had a terrace that ran around the exterior of the property and crimson bougainvillaea clung to the walls. A plethora of freesias bordered the pathway to the front entrance which infused the atmosphere with an aromatic perfume. It was like something from a romantic movie that took my breath away.

Inside was just as stunning – there were marble floors throughout with Persian rugs scattered everywhere and a huge sixty-foot lounge decked out with antique furniture. The kitchen was top of the range for its time, and there were five ensuite bedrooms which were rare in the seventies. Dave and I had a four-poster bed with blue silk drapes. I loved it, however, it was so high to climb onto, I needed a stool, and George had to come and help launch Dave onto the bed. It was quite comical.

Being fiesta time, many of the men were busy collecting wood from the huge grounds to put on the large bonfire. There were around ten of us merry-making with the Portuguese neighbours exchanging our language differences. Most people, including Dave, were all sitting around the fire singing, guitar strumming, drinking, and smoking. I sat further back in the garden chatting with a couple of guys.

The bonfire needed refuelling, but I was too busy talking when I heard my name being shouted. I'd only taken my eyes off Dave for a few minutes, so I hadn't noticed that he'd been loaded up with branches by one of the Portuguese guys. They were wedged into the crook of his spastic arms and as he attempted to throw the wood onto the dying embers, he'd lost his balance and landed face down in the fire, the branches still lodged into his arms.

"Mary, you better come quickly. Dave's fallen in the fire," someone shouted.

It must have been well past midnight as I stood up panic-stricken, seeing two guys pulling him out from the flames. As I rushed forward, they had him upright, holding onto him on each side as he staggered forward.

Desperately worried about how badly he may have been burnt, I could instantly see that his beard was singed, and the rest of his face looked bright red. But worse, both his arms and hands looked severely burnt with the skin turning black and peeling off. Dave didn't say a word, he just stood there shaking, clearly in shock.

"Someone, please, call an ambulance," I screamed, glancing around.

Everyone was slow to respond as it was late, we'd all had a few joints and quite a bit to drink. Then one of the guys holding onto him said in broken English, "It will take ages for an ambulance to get here. We're too remote."

Fortunately, our sober host, George, added, "Don't worry, get him in the car and I'll drive you both to the hospital."

I thanked him and took a deep breath. I should have taken it all in my stride by then, knowing that in Dave's struggle to be independent, he regularly put himself in danger. But I was a nervous wreck.

The drive took a good thirty minutes as we headed down windy dark lanes towards the hospital in Lisbon. I sat with Dave in the back of the car, trying not to touch any of his burnt skin, and put my hand on his leg to reassure him. "It'll be all right, it'll be all right," I repeated, attempting to comfort both of us.

On arrival, we headed to A & E where nurses whisked him away on a trolley. All we could do was wait. Hours later, as the sun was rising, we were told Dave was on a ward. When we were finally allowed to see him, there was gauze on his forehead and his hands and arms were bandaged up. He remained there for a couple of days, so we had to extend our two-week stay by another week. But by the time we returned home his skin was already healing. He really was a survivor.

CHAPTER TWENTY-TWO

Onwards and Upwards

At the end of those two years of Dave's rehab, I was informed by medics that there was nothing more they could do for him. He still needed to work on his speech and still needed to balance more when he walked. We both felt disillusioned, but a friend gave us hope when she told us of a new place in Cheltenham called The Traditional Chinese Acupuncture Clinic which was having rave reviews.

Initially, Dave was doubtful about it. "How can sticking needles in me make me feel better?" he stuttered between grunts and gasps. And I was realistic, I knew they couldn't work miracles, but we were grasping at straws, thinking it might help his immune system and wellbeing. And Dave was desperate to get back to the man he used to be.

That was the beginning of a lifelong friendship with Mike Eatough, the acupuncturist and Maggie, his Scottish girlfriend who worked as a reflexologist in the same clinic. We couldn't afford much, but Mike told us upfront that we could donate whatever we could afford. And in truth, I was grateful as both Dave and I needed support to cope physically and mentally with the new journey we were on.

Mike saw Dave for weekly sessions using acupuncture to stimulate his meridians in different parts of his body to help the 'Chi' energy flow whilst Maggie introduced me to meditation and The Metamorphic

Technique which is derived from Reflexology, lightly touching the meridians of the foot, rather than the usual firm pressure. It definitely helped me to destress and relax a little more.

Over the months, Dave had a huge improvement. He was walking more upright, and the muscles in his arm weren't as contorted. Even his speech improved – but more importantly than all of that, it gave him a sense of inner peace.

Inner peace was also something I'd been missing. I'd stayed strong and coped as well as I could, but one evening, I fell to pieces. I was in our living room, curled up sobbing on the sofa, shaking and crying. I didn't know why or what was happening to me but in hindsight, it must have been a breakdown. Dave was sitting next to me. "I wish I knew what to do to help you?" he said, reaching out his hand to touch my shoulder.

I was so distressed, I couldn't speak, so he suggested we ring Maggie and Mike. They immediately came over to give me an acupuncture treatment. I lay on the bed as Mike put the needles in and Maggie held my hand saying, "Breathe. It's going to be all right." And afterwards, I felt so much calmer.

Mike explained that this was all part and parcel of the treatment I'd had resulting in an emotional and physical detox. There was a lot of delayed trauma where I'd had to keep being strong whilst painting on a smile to help Dave. Naturally, I didn't have the physical injuries that Dave experienced, but my inner pain wasn't quite so easy to heal. The couple told me that they'd always support me through any issue, and I was glad to have some answers as to why my feelings were so overwhelming.

Those eastern techniques opened up a whole new world and I learned a lot from Mike and Maggie about Tibetan Buddhism and the Dalai Lama. All these years later, I still follow the philosophy and use a mantra in my daily meditation.

PART 4

JIM

Wise men say
Only fools rush in
But I can't help falling in love with you
Shall I stay?
Would it be a sin?
If I can't help falling in love with you

CHAPTER TWENTY-THREE

1982 – A Fork in the Road

Maggie, the reflexologist, and Ann, another acupuncturist booked a three-bed self-catering apartment in Ibiza for a week and asked if I'd like to join them. Having given up smoking for a year, I'd saved the cigarette money in a jar, so there were enough pounds, shillings, and pence for me to yell, "Yes, please."

The truth was, I was desperate for a break, and deep down, although I always wore a smile, I wasn't happy. And why would I be? I was still a young woman – thirty-one years old – and the last eight years of my life were split between running a shop and caring for a disabled person with no time for my own needs.

Then, it seemed, fate had a new plan in store.

Maggie, Ann, and I were sitting outside a restaurant on Callalonga Beach having wine and nibbles in the sunshine when we noticed two guys at a nearby table. Maggie being Scottish, overheard one of the guys had a familiar brogue. In an enthusiastic holiday mood, she leaned towards them and said, "Boys, would you like to join us?"

My eyes lit up. I could tell they were young lads, and I was up for a laugh after all the stress. They immediately came over, introducing themselves as Jim and Ian from Glasgow. I soon discovered that Jim, a slim, tanned, and blond twenty-two-year-old, worked as a jeweller. Ian was also the same age, fair-haired and a photographer. They were staying in San Antonio for two weeks.

Both boys were chatting animatedly to Maggie and Ann, so feeling a bit left out, I asked if I could take a spin on one of their motorbikes that were parked up nearby. Jim leapt off his seat as if he was on fire, and said, "Sure, hop on."

I wondered if he thought I wanted him to take me, so to make a point, I jumped on one of the bikes and started it up. He then got on the other bike and sped after me, and we rode up and down the beach laughing our heads off.

Maggie invited them both back to ours for dinner and after another wine fuelled meal of lasagne, we all went skinny dipping in the moonlight on the beach right outside our apartment. I admit skinny dipping was my idea. I was tipsy and feeling hot and reckless, so we all stripped off, leaving our clothes on the shore, except for Maggie who sat on the sand watching us wade into the sea in our birthday suits.

Initially, we were all laughing and splashing each other, and then Jim and I started spontaneously kissing. I'd previously just thought of him as a fun-loving youngster, but suddenly, that kiss ignited something, and I really got the hots for him.

The two of us held hands as we waded back to the beach, dripping wet, and pulled our clothes back on over damp skin.

Heading back to the apartment, Jim ended up in my bed as we kissed and cuddled. But I was still a married woman, so we didn't make love. I thought no harm done, it's just a bit of much-needed affection.

In the morning, after a quick coffee, Jim and his friend, Ian, who'd seemingly got together with Ann, both said their goodbyes. Jim left me the hotel telephone number where he was staying, and with butterflies in my tummy, I couldn't help but wonder if he'd really want to meet up with me again. After all, I was nine years older than him – but he'd left a lasting effect on me, and as naive as it might sound, I felt like a giddy teenager.

After the boys had gone, Maggie and Ann asked if I wanted to go to one of the local markets, but I just wanted to stay in and sort my head out. Once alone, I paced the floor restlessly, reflecting on how this new guy had thrown my life with Dave up into the air. On the flight over, I'd read my horoscope in an in-flight magazine, and it spoke of pastures new, and leaving and meeting a new man! Was Jim that new man? All I knew is that I hadn't felt like this since the first heady days of meeting Dave.

I needed to know if the night before had meant something to Jim too, but I continued to pace the apartment, agonising over whether to call him or not. Then I noticed that he'd left behind a gold dagger earring on the bedside cabinet. Let's just say, that was a good excuse to ring without seeming desperate. So, I ran down to the telephone kiosk outside the hotel and called.

"Hey, you," he said on answering the phone, "Why don't you come on over and we'll head to a nightclub later."

I was thrilled that he seemed pleased to hear from me and the next three days were a crazy whirlwind – moonlit walks on the beach, heading out to restaurants in a lovesick trance, totally wrapped up in one another as we held hands and gazed into each other's eyes, and then, making love all night.

It was such a contrast to what I'd been used to. My life with Dave was in all honesty, pretty humdrum. I'd become an old lady before my time, returning from work to sit in front of the telly with him, a tray of food on our laps, as we chatted about the notorious Sue Ellen from *Dallas* who kept her gin in a perfume bottle. And to get down to the nitty-gritty, sex was out of the question. Sure, we slept together in the same bed, and I kissed and cuddled him as much as I could with one of his contracted arms still sticking out – but when we did try, which was rare, the act itself was always fumbling and awkward, and not remotely enjoyable.

In a restaurant overlooking the sea, I'd confided in Jim about my marriage. He was still living at home with his mum and at the very start of his life adventures. Despite our age differences and the challenges involved, he looked deeply into my eyes and said, "I've fallen for you, Mary. The only problem is I'm single and you're married, so what now?"

I told him, I felt the same, but it was all so overwhelming. I wanted to move forward, but I didn't want to hurt Dave, so, what was I going to do? Because after a taste of this new life, I couldn't face going back to my mundane routine at home.

Initially, Jim and I considered running away from everything by getting bar work in Ibiza, but when we discussed it with Maggie and Ann, they both said, no way, you've got to go back and face the music. They were older and wiser than me, and I guess they felt I had to take responsibility. But I was scared. Although it may sound selfish, I was worried if I went back that I'd be forced to stay.

Jim headed home on his flight a day later. I had his contact details at work as well as his mum's house phone number and we pledged to get back in touch and make a decision. But deep down, I'd already made a decision – I'd confess everything to Dave and then pack up for Scotland and start afresh. It might seem rash as I barely knew this guy and I had no idea if it was just a holiday fling that would fizzle out, but that was fine with me – if nothing else, Jim might just be the catalyst for me to move forward.

After getting off the morning flight, instead of heading home, I drove to Carolyn's cottage. She knew me better than anyone, witnessing all the challenges I'd been through, and I needed her insight on my sudden life decision.

"I just don't know what to do, Car," I said, sitting down at her kitchen table and wringing my hands. "Should I stay with Dave or take the fall out and leave?"

Whilst she put the kettle on, Carolyn sat down opposite me. "You know what, Mary, you've made a huge sacrifice in marrying Dave, putting your own life on hold, and I haven't seen you this happy for a long time. Follow your instincts. I think going for what you want is the right thing to do."

When I left her place, I was in no doubt, that I had to pluck up the courage to tell Dave the truth.

CHAPTER TWENTY-FOUR

Finding Courage and Faith

Arriving back at the flat I shared with Dave, I dumped my suitcase in the hallway and walked into the living room to find the place filled with huge bouquets. I felt a surge of guilt as Dave walked towards me with a smile. "I've missed you desperately," he said, reaching his arms out for a hug.

I was sick with nerves, having palpitations, knowing I was about to drop this huge bombshell that would change both our lives forever. But I had to say it before I exploded. Looking him straight in the eye, I blurted out, "Dave, I've met someone on holiday. I'm in love and I'm going to move up to Scotland to be with him."

I must have said it with such conviction because he didn't try and plead with me. Instead, he was speechless with a look of forlorn disbelief probably wondering how this had all happened in the space of a week.

I kept saying sorry over and over, but I was shaking and couldn't stay there a moment longer after what I'd said and done, having been unfaithful whilst we were still married. "I better go," I said, as I walked towards the hallway. "I'm staying with Carolyn overnight, so I'll get my stuff in the morning."

The next day, Carolyn returned to the flat with me and I collected a few belongings as well as some treasured knick-knacks: some silver matchboxes and spoons, a wooden Tumbridge Wells sewing box, and a London Aerodrome Trophy given to the winner of the flying competitions between 1911 and 1914.

Dave wasn't in, and frankly, I was relieved not to have any intense conversations where he might break down and cry. Looking back, I think he stayed out because he couldn't bear to see me leave either.

After Carolyn and I left, I drove to my mother's place to explain my momentous decision. I didn't have to contend with dad as he'd been dead for three years. I loved him dearly, despite our misunderstandings, but I could just imagine him hollering down from the sky, "Divorce is a sin." Although I'm grateful he mellowed as he got older, and we healed our rift before he passed.

However, Mum was distraught after I told her my plan and began to cry. "What! How can you just up sticks and go?" she said between sobs. "What about Dave?"

I touched her hand. "Mum, I know it's hard, but it'll be the best thing for Dave. I do everything for him and he's too dependent on me and getting old before his time."

After lots of talking, she knew I wouldn't change my mind having made my own way since I was seventeen.

With a thumping heart, I drove Carolyn back to the cottage and then found a phone box on the roadside. I rang Jim at work to arrange to meet him at the Smugglers Rest in Glasgow and then began my seven-hour drive to Scotland.

CHAPTER TWENTY-FIVE

A New Pathway

It was around 6 p.m. when Jim rushed into the pub after work and pulled me into his arms. "You came, you actually came," I gasped as I hugged him.

"Of course, I came," he replied with a twinkle in his eyes, "I'm madly in love with you."

I gazed at him, still feeling the same intense emotions, my heart thumping like mad. Some people might say I was brave or stupid, but the fact is, I had no idea where we were going to stay that night. And I didn't care as long as we were together.

Over a drink in the pub, we decided to book a B & B for three nights until we found something more permanent. Naturally not everyone agreed with our decision because let's face it, on paper, it sounded crazy. Jim told his mother that he'd met this married older woman and we were going to move in together, and apparently, she was fuming, ranting at him down the phone. I don't blame her. His dad had died the year before and she thought he was setting himself up for disaster. I could understand her worries, after all, he was her wee boy, and I probably seemed like some Mrs Robinson type who'd seduce him and then toss him aside.

The next morning, when Jim went off to work, I looked for a flat to rent as it was obvious by his mother's reaction that we couldn't go back there. One of his friends gave us a contact of an Italian café owner who seemed to be a bit of a property entrepreneur, so I went to see him. He took me round the corner to check out a bedsit up six flights of stairs, a bargain for ten pounds a week. It was what you called a tenement with no bath or shower, only a sink, but we were desperate and at least it was our place where we could relax and be ourselves. Besides, Jim could always have a bath at his mum's, and I could shower at the tanning salon or the swimming baths.

Realistically, though, it was hugely inconvenient, so after a few weeks, I went back and asked Mr Café Owner if he had another place with a bathroom. Fortunately, he did, and we moved into an upgraded bedsit.

Here's another letter I wrote to my brother at the time explaining everything.

25th September 1982

Dear Pat and Jean,

Well, here I am sitting in our little flat – happy, contented and feeling, at last, at peace. I know that someday, I was going to do what I have done but not quite like this. I've spent far too long smiling on the outside and crying inwardly. Everyone will be okay, I know that. Carolyn has been in touch with Dave and apparently, he's coping well. It will be the making of him to finally stand on his own two feet.

Mum, well she's in the middle of her move, so at least she's got that to take her mind off things. (Mum had sold her council house and bought a ground-floor flat in Bourton on the Water).

Me, well, I'm very happy here. The Glaswegians are lovely, and Glasgow is just about big enough for me. I'm lost in a mass of people who don't know me – Heaven! So, I'm copping out and it's wonderful.

Jim, the guy who whisked me off my feet in Ibiza is lovely – very gentle, kind and very, very loving. Just what the doctor ordered. I'm happy for as long as it lasts. I'm going to make the most of it. We went to Loch Lomand the other week – beautiful – the countryside is fabulous. Edinburgh is also a lovely city. We wouldn't mind moving there – still, we'll see. If our plans work out, we hope to be doing a lot of things. Jim is just about due home now and dinner is cooking (is this really me?) so I'll go see to it.

Just a short letter to let you know my address and that I'm fine. I feel eighteen again, and at last, I can breathe. I'm looking for work but had no luck yet. Still, only been here for two weeks. Something will turn up. We're off swimming tonight. We've got a two-room flat up six flights of stairs so I'm getting super fit.
My love and happiness to you both,
Mary xxxx

Three months later, I still hadn't told Dave or even my mother where I was. As selfish as that may sound, knowing they'd all be worried sick, I was scared they might put the kibosh on my newly found happiness.

But the past soon caught up with me …

I got a job washing up in a café and was in the kitchen when one of the waitresses came in and said, "Mary, there's a man in a suit drinking coffee. He's asked if a Mary Browning works here?"

My stomach flipped over. I felt like a criminal on the run. Who the hell knew my name and what did they want? I dried my hands on a tea towel and nervously wandered through the café. I instantly clocked a grey-haired man at one of the tables by the window. Walking over to him, I sat down opposite, my throat tightening. "Hello, I'm Mary Browning. You've been asking about me?" I said, studying him with narrowed eyes.

He leaned forward, his expression serious. "Yes, thank you for agreeing to talk to me. I'm a private investigator. Your husband Dave hired me to find you."

My mouth dropped open. "Dave hired a PI to find me?" I repeated.

He took a slurp of coffee. "Yes, naturally, he, and all your family and friends want you back home safe and sound."

I felt a rush of anxiety. "I'm not going back," I snapped. "I've made a new life here now."

The PI gave a tight smile. "Well, can I at least pass on your address, so they know where you are?"

"No!" I said adamantly, "I'm not giving it to you." I had visions of a crowd of them banging on my door and forcibly hauling me back home.

He nodded in acceptance, clearly seeing it was impossible to convince me otherwise. "Well, they'll be disappointed, but I'll write up a report and give my response." And then he got up and left.

When I went home that evening, I told Jim what had happened and we hugged each other even more tightly, feeling like illicit lovers. Both of us were a jittery mess whenever we heard a knock on the front door or someone walking up the stairs, thinking that Dave had employed someone to stalk and kidnap me. It brought us even closer, knowing we couldn't bear to lose each other.

CHAPTER TWENTY-SIX

Second Time Around

As the years sped by, I wanted to be free to marry Jim, but I had to wait a long time before I could finally be liberated from my marital status. I filed the divorce papers, but Dave kept contesting it. I was frustrated with him wondering why he couldn't just move on and let me go, but thankfully, there was a legal loophole – after five years the divorce could go ahead without his consent as we'd already been separated. The proviso was that Dave got to keep our flat.

During that time, I'd gone up in the world, leaving my job at the café to become manageress of one of the hottest stores in town that showcased outfits from all the top designers. It was one hundred and ten pounds a week which was a sharp contrast to the rubbish forty pounds a week salary I was on in the cafe. Jim was also on good money, so, we moved out of the grotty bedsit and bought a one-bed flat in Glasgow for fifteen thousand pounds.

Eventually, though, I got bored with fashion and flicking through the local paper one evening, I saw an advert for couples to become pub managers in London. It instantly sparked my interest as I was keen to do something completely different. I'd always loved London – plus it meant free accommodation and food.

Jim was always up for something new and immediately said with a grin, "Sure, let's do it." I was relieved he shared the same mindset as me. After all, what did either of us have to lose?

I sent off the application and discovered they were holding interviews in Glasgow.

Success! Only a few weeks later, we'd rented out our flat, sold our MG, and headed off to London to train for nine months to become pub managers – I learned to cook for sixty people a day, and we became familiar with bar work and dealing with all the beer and ale that was kept in kegs in the cellar. We also had to order stock as well as take responsibility for cashing up and the weekly accounts.

After the training was completed, we were assigned our very own pub – the Bricklayers Arms – and we loved every minute of it. In fact, it became our career for the next ten years. In that industry, the social circle at work becomes your life, so we built up a close group of friends that we met over the bar.

We lived for adventure, travelling all over the world on our holidays, and going to nightclubs and late-night shows. It was a freedom I'd never felt before, to feel that I was fully embracing life with a like-minded partner.

Thankfully, by then, his mum had grown to love me, always hugging me when she saw me and saying, "You're like a daughter to me." I was touched when she gave me a half sovereign on a gold chain that had been in the family for years. She had three of them and the others were given to her two daughters, so I treasured being made to feel like one of the family.

1989 – I'm Getting Married in the Morning

I finally got hitched to Jim in Camden registry office. All we wanted was to commit ourselves to each other with no pressure, so our wedding was an intimate affair with only two other couples – Dave and Moira who regularly frequented the pub where we often had lock-ins, especially on a Friday night. And then there were Ozzie backpackers, Helen and Steve, who we employed to work behind the bar.

Of course, I wanted to let loved ones know that we'd finally tied the knot, so, afterwards, we planned a two-week honeymoon to drive around and see all my family and friends face to face.

I'd always kept in touch with most of my family and friends by letter, but it was wonderful to finally catch up with my brother, Pat and his wife Jean, Mike the acupuncturist and his partner Maggie, my friend Carolyn, and of course my dear mother. Everyone was over the moon for us, except that my mother was disappointed that she hadn't witnessed her only daughter getting married, but she understood. Naturally, we didn't feel it was appropriate to visit Dave. Jim wouldn't have been comfortable meeting my ex-husband, given the circumstances of how we met.

CHAPTER TWENTY-SEVEN

1998 – Reunited And it Feels So Good

With great sadness, I attended my friend Maggie's funeral. She'd died of a massive brain haemorrhage whilst driving her car. Mike had called me with the news. I was devastated. She'd been such a huge part of my own healing journey that it was like missing a limb.

I went on my own without Jim as he didn't know most of the people attending. Then as I stood in a crowd of mourners after the service had finished, I heard a familiar voice. "Doodles, Doodles." I turned around and saw Dave, standing there in a suit with his cheeky grin. My heart stopped. I had so many mixed emotions – grief at losing my dear friend, Maggie, and then seeing one of the most significant men from my past for the first time in nine years.

I hugged him, pleased to see him doing so well, and he gave me an update on everything that happened to him. It was hard to hear that it had taken him several years to get over me leaving, but I knew being without me would make him more autonomous. I was also proud to hear that he'd attended a creative writing workshop as well as becoming an integral part of 'Headway Cotswold' helping others who'd experienced head injuries. He'd also learnt to use a word processor with his functioning hand and was now in a relationship with one of the helpers at the Day Centre he attended, round the corner from where he lived.

Mike, Maggie's partner, suddenly appeared amidst the crowds of people and without any words spoken, all three of us hugged each other, sobbed, and then looked up at the sky.

"Maggie, you've done it again," I said. "You've reunited us all." She was always so good at playing peacemaker.

CHAPTER TWENTY-EIGHT

2000 – Healing and Closure

When my mother turned eighty-two, despite being in a wheelchair, she came to stay with Jim and me for her birthday. By this time, we moved to a bungalow in Suffolk to manage 'The Crown Pub'. We celebrated in a local tavern, but when we wheeled mum back home, she was a little tipsy, so I moved her into the lounge and said, "Stay there, don't move. I'll make us all a cuppa."

Jim went outside to have a cigarette, so she was left alone for five minutes. I came back into the lounge to find her lying on the living room floor crying out in pain. It seems that she'd tried to clamber out of her wheelchair and onto the sofa and fell.

In a flurry, I called an ambulance, and she was taken to hospital where they diagnosed a broken hip. She remained there for a month until she died of pneumonia. I was devastated. It took me a long time to get over her death as I blamed myself for leaving her alone.

Suddenly, I felt the compelling need to see Dave and tell him about Mum. They'd always been close and still met up after I'd left, so I wanted to find solace in someone who'd known her well. Plus, I'd always felt guilty about abandoning him and hadn't addressed that when I met him at Maggie's funeral. We didn't have much time and there were so many people around. But now, two years on, I felt as if closure was needed.

Knocking on the door of my former home, I felt sick with nerves, taking deep breaths, not knowing how Dave would react or if his girlfriend was there with him.

When he opened the door, he stood staring at me, speechless, as if he was wondering if I was real or not. Then he stepped forward and hugged me tight, and we stayed like that for a few moments, sobbing our hearts out.

He invited me in, and we stood in my old kitchen that I knew so well whilst he put the kettle on. Although, it had only been two years ago that I'd seen him at Maggie's funeral, he looked older and was struggling to walk, holding onto things to keep his balance. Naturally, I looked older too. At the age of fifty, my hair had turned white, and I had a few more laughter lines around my eyes.

We talked about our lives, and I mentioned what Jim and I had been up to, and he told me that he was still in the same relationship. He appeared to be doing amazingly well. In that strange circle of life, he'd met up with Steve who'd first introduced us on Christmas Eve nearly thirty years ago. Steve was now racing a Formula Ford car with his brothers and Dave had become their timekeeper and a big part of the team. He'd also accepted a reporter's job with the Monoposto club's monthly magazine, *Starline*, covering events at Mallory Park, Thruxton, Silverstone, and Castle Combe. His eyes lit up as he talked about it, and I could see how much he relished being back in the world he loved. Even more admirable, he'd been awarded the Quill Trophy for his autobiography, *Seven Springs*, which documented his accident and his life before and after. In 1998, an extract of Dave's autobiography was read by one of his friends at the Cheltenham Literary Festival. I felt so proud to hear of his incredible accomplishments considering all that he'd been through.

"You know," he said looking at me with a soft smile, "winning that trophy gave me the same buzz as being given my two silver replicas in the 1970 and 1971 Isle of Man T.T. races." He paused. "Well, almost!" he added with a chuckle. He picked up the kettle and poured some hot water into a teapot. "Anyway, with what do I owe this unexpected pleasure? Is everything okay with Jim?"

"Yes, we're good thanks." After a deep breath, I plucked up the courage to tell him the reason why I'd come. "Mum's dead," I blurted out, my eyes filling with tears.

Dave froze for a moment and then hugged me again. "Oh, no, I'm so sorry, Doodles," he said softly, "she was a very special lady who really helped me heal after you left."

Oh God, there was that stab of guilt again.

I then did something I'd rehearsed a thousand times over the years. I looked him square in the eyes and said, "Dave, I'm so sorry for everything …. for abandoning you, for not letting you know where I'd gone …"

"Doodles, it's fine," he interrupted as he touched my arm. "I'm grateful for all the years you gave me after the accident. Not many would have done what you did. And you deserve to be happy, so there's nothing to feel sorry about."

And with that, my eyes welled up again. His acceptance was a great unburdening; removal of the ton of guilt I'd been carrying all these years.

And for the first time, I felt truly free.

EPILOGUE

In the summer of 2022, at the age of seventy-one, I've said my goodbyes to many loved ones, and I feel lucky to still be here. Although I have several autoimmune diseases that might slow me down a little, I'm still raring to go with the same spirit of adventure that I've always had. Even if I've slipped up along the way, and made mistakes, I've always had faith that things will get better.

And forty years later, I'm still married to Jim, and I know that there are more adventures to come. I've already gone up in a hot air balloon, flown a glider, a helicopter, and a two-seater plane with an instructor. But I still have some exciting goals.

I plan to do a parachute jump. And I still want to get back in a racing car and have a few more laps around Brands Hatch!

In Loving Memory of Lynne

Lynne made many attempts to end her life and this increased after her mother died. Having a baby settled her down for a while, but Dave's accident and her father's death tipped her over the edge. After two attempts to drive her car off a bridge and miraculously surviving, in May 1978, she eventually jumped off a bridge onto a railway track, dying instantly, leaving behind her devoted husband and much longed-for son. The coroner's report stated: Accidental death while the balance of her mind was disturbed.

I missed Lynne hugely. She'd become a big part of our life and although she suffered from severe depression, ironically, I did miss her humour and support. She'd give me some much-needed time out by looking after Dave, and she was also hugely giving.

After her funeral in 1978, I did my best to support her husband by babysitting their little boy, so Mervin could get out for a night. I felt so sorry for the poor guy. He was Lynne's rock who stuck by her through all her ups and downs. And he never remarried.

In Loving Memory of Mike

In June 2021, my dearest friend, Mike, the acupuncturist, died at the age of ninety-five. He'd continued to run the acupuncture clinic after Maggie died for some time. It was the end of an era for me. His words of wisdom, his penetrating eyes, and his comforting bear hugs are still with me today. Whenever I visited Cheltenham, I always made plans to see him in his motor home overlooking a field of horses in Little Witcombe, just outside Cheltenham. We often meditated together and counted our many blessings with gratitude. He was an extraordinary man full of stories, laughter, and a deep sense of compassion and knowledge.

In Loving Memory of Dave

In April 2004, Dave's eldest son, Mark, rang me to tell me that his father had suffered a heart attack and died at home during the night. "Oh goodness, I'm so sorry," I stuttered not knowing how to respond.

I immediately packed some things and drove off to Carolyn's. I was desperate to go to the funeral at Bethesda Methodist Church. I wanted to say my final goodbye to this inspirational man, and I needed my bestie for moral support. After all, I hadn't seen any of our mutual friends since 1981! Would they still see me as 'that bitch' that abandoned my disabled husband after seven years of marriage?

I needn't have worried. It was a wonderful gathering full of light and love. I finally met Lynne's son, now a tall, dark, and handsome man in his twenties. And his father, Merv looked much the same, except he was a little bit plumper. There was still no lady with him. He never wanted anyone else but Lynne.

Dave's stepmother, Carol was married again, although she'd come to the funeral alone. We were happy to see each other, hugging tightly.

I said a heartfelt farewell as Dave's coffin swished behind the curtains.

Goodbye Dave, wherever you are. You made a huge impact on my life. And for that, I am eternally grateful.